30-MINUTE GROUPS

MANAGING BIG EMOTIONS

IDENTIFYING TRIGGERS, DEVELOPING COPING STRATEGIES, AND COMMUNICATING EFFECTIVELY

GINGER HEALY

NATIONAL CENTER for YOUTH ISSUES

Duplication and Copyright

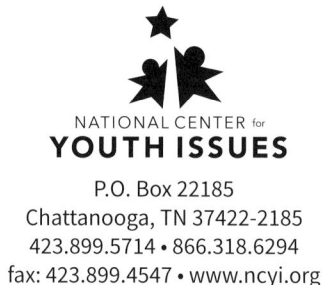

NATIONAL CENTER for YOUTH ISSUES

P.O. Box 22185
Chattanooga, TN 37422-2185
423.899.5714 • 866.318.6294
fax: 423.899.4547 • www.ncyi.org

ISBN: 9781965066027

© 2024 National Center for Youth Issues, Chattanooga, TN

All rights reserved.

Written by: Ginger Healy

Published by National Center for Youth Issues

Printed in the U.S.A. • August 2025

Third party links are accurate at the time of publication, but may change over time.

The information in this book is designed to provide helpful information on the subjects discussed and is not intended to be used, nor should it be used, to diagnose or treat any mental health or medical condition. For diagnosis or treatment of any mental health or medical issue, consult a licensed counselor, psychologist, or physician. The publisher and author are not responsible for any specific mental or physical health needs that may require medical supervision, and are not liable for any damages or negative consequences from any treatment, action, application, or preparation, to any person reading or following the information in this book. References are provided for informational purposes only and do not constitute endorsement of any websites or other sources.

ASCA National Model®, Recognized ASCA Model Program® and RAMP® are registered trademarks of the American School Counselor Association. Our use of them does not imply an affiliation with or endorsement by the American School Counselor Association.

Portions of this workbook were adapted with permission from the
Kids with Character series by Maureen Duran ©NCYI 1995. All rights reserved.

Contents

Introduction

Knowing how to manage big emotions will help children throughout their lives. The goal isn't to eliminate all feelings but to lean into them, figure out where they are coming from, and then learn to manage them. These skills take a long time to learn, but the learning path can be filled with safe and positive relationships that help students build resilience.

This Managing Big Emotions curriculum is tailored for 2nd through 8th graders and consists of ten to twelve thirty-minute lessons to help students learn how to navigate overwhelming feelings. The goal is to help students learn emotional regulation skills that lead to regulated nervous systems, stronger and safer relationships, and greater resilience. This curriculum recognizes the unique ways in which each student learns, emphasizing that there's no singular 'correct' way to embrace these ideas. Just as each lesson is individualized to cater to diverse learning styles, the curriculum remains flexible, ensuring that every child can engage, understand, and practice these essential regulation skills.

The strategic design allows students to empathize, connect with others, and translate their new knowledge into practice. The American School Counselor Association (ASCA®)-aligned curriculum contains an introductory lesson, ten core lessons, and a final closing lesson. Facilitators have the flexibility to include the initial and final lessons as part of the core sessions if they have extra time.

You'll find a range of essential resources in the book's concluding pages. These consist of permission and completion letters, attendance logs, a group expectation form, and a certificate of completion. You'll also find pre- and post-group surveys to measure the success of the programming and templates to share the results with interested parties. Moreover, this workbook provides a comprehensive small group action plan that will integrate effortlessly into your ASCA® evaluation document and facilitate a seamless transition from planning to assessment.

Practical and applicable, the activities provided are suitable for small and large group instruction and require no additional materials. You do not need to bring supplies beyond pencils, markers or crayons, and scratch paper; you won't need to spend hours prepping materials before meeting with your students. Everything you need is included!

See page 79 for information on Downloadable Resources.

What's Included?

Managing Big Emotions offers a comprehensive ten-lesson program and accompanying materials for facilitating group sessions. Following each detailed lesson outline, you'll find practical resources for establishing a small group within your school environment.

Mind Map: Provides an illustrated diagram of the regulation skill that can help students make connections between the regulation concept and other concepts. Students should begin each lesson by considering the meaning of the specific regulation skill. It is optional to write these, but visuals are helpful for many students. Some have found it helpful to draw the Mind Map on the board, or you can draw a tree with the concept written on the trunk and the related words on the fruit on the tree.

ASCA® Standards: Each lesson includes success criteria for the learning target.

Lesson Introduction: At the start of each lesson, we will introduce a concept and explain it to provide clarity for the upcoming story.

Circle Time Questions: This section has three optional questions for the facilitator to start the conversation. These questions allow students to deepen their understanding of the topic and build community by discussing and sharing their experiences.

Story Time: Provides stories related to the concept that should be read aloud to help children understand the concept.

Coloring Sheets: Allow students to visualize the concept. Students can color the sheet while the facilitator shares the initial story after the lesson is complete or take it home with them.

Discussion Questions: Students can discuss the questions posed to help them process their beliefs on the subject.

Skill Practice: Using the round-robin method, go around the table and ask students how they would practice that skill, giving each a chance to answer one question.

Additional Activities: Provides activities to help students practice and apply the concept.

Closing Considerations: Is an opportunity to review the concept and ask students to reflect on their new experience with the material.

Would You Rather? Game: Provides an opportunity for students to consider what they would "rather" do related to the lesson's topic. The facilitator can cut out the cards and let students discuss or read aloud while moving from one side of the room to the other to communicate their preferred answer.

Accompanying Group Documents

Small Group Action Plan Guide: Provides the necessary information required to complete the ASCA® National Model's Small Group Action Plan.

Permission Form: The permission form is used to gain the permission of the student's caregivers for the child to attend the Managing Big Emotions group. Be sure to send this home about two weeks before the group starts.

Group Expectations: These provide basic expectations for the group process. The form has space for the facilitator and group to collaborate on adding additional expectations to fit their group.

Group Attendance Form: This is a blank form that allows the facilitator to track which students attended each session and what topics were discussed.

Group Attendance Form (Example): This form is an example of how to best utilize the group attendance form.

Pre- and Post-Group Survey: Provides an opportunity for students to share what they know of the concepts before and after they've completed the curriculum.

To measure the progress of students who participate, use the same assessment for both the pre-group and post-group survey. Administer the pre-group survey at the start of the instructional period, followed by instruction and practice opportunities for measured skills or knowledge.

At the end of the instructional period, administer the post-survey and compare the results of both surveys to identify areas of improvement and areas that need further instruction. Then calculate the average score of the pre-survey and post-survey and determine the percentage of improvement by subtracting the pre-survey average from the post-survey average and then dividing the result by the pre-survey average. Use this pre-survey average improvement to measure the students' progress effectively.

Percentage of Improvement Formula:
((Post-Group Total - Pre-Group Total) / Pre-Group Total)) x 100 = Percentage of Overall Improvement

Example:
((31 Post Group Total - 19 Pre-Group Total) / 19) x 100 = 63.15% Overall Improvement

Look at your data to determine who should attend your group. Review conduct referrals, attendance data, and achievement metrics and look for students with deficits. Consider also tracking students' academic achievements, absences, and discipline referrals. You can better see the impact of your small groups when strategically selecting students and closely monitoring their academic, attendance, and conduct metrics. Be sure to share the results of your intervention with your advisory council.

Post-Group Survey Results: The survey shows one way to share your data with your interested parties. Remember, we want to make sure that we use graphs and charts as they show our data, which is often more impactful than a paragraph of text. Use whatever platform you prefer to show your data but be sure to complete the data following the group and then share with your interested parties.

Post-Group Survey Results (Example): The survey shows what your data might resemble following the completion of the groups. You can use this form to share your data.

Certificate of Completion: Present students with a certificate to congratulate them on completing the curriculum.

Managing Big Emotions Group Completion Letter: Letter written to the caregivers/guardians of students following the completion of the group. Provide students with their certificate and their group review letter during the last session.

Additional Materials: We promised to provide everything you need in this workbook, and we have. However, you will need to make copies of the pre- and post-group assessment surveys and print the coloring pages. You might also print and cut the "Would You Rather?" game or facilitate that activity verbally. We recommend having crayons or colored pencils readily available on the table for those who wish to complete the coloring sheet. It might also be helpful to have some fidgets accessible for your students during their group session.

Good luck with your group! We hope you have a fantastic experience!

Introductory Group Session

Directions & Overview

Conduct this introductory session before starting the regular lessons. This initial meeting will acclimate students to the program's structure, expectations, and foundational tools. They will learn the brain model and check-in process that will be utilized in each subsequent session.

Directions: Begin by extending a warm welcome to all participants. Communicate the group's objectives and generate enthusiasm for learning and collaboration.

Survey: Before proceeding, read the pre-group survey instructions aloud to the students and have each student complete the form. Carefully examine the completed forms to verify that all questions have been answered.

Introductions: Foster a sense of community by encouraging students to share their names, something about themselves, and what they wish to learn in the group. Share that they will be asked to do the "brain stoplight check-in" during each session. Explain how it works and practice that check-in now. (It is important to demonstrate the hand model of the brain before teaching the check-in.)

When the hand is closed in a gentle fist with fingers over the thumb, it represents a calm and flexible brain where we can make good decisions even if we are upset. Notice how the fingers touch the thumb. This means the top part of the brain is helping control emotions. Sometimes, those feelings get so big that we flip our lid. The fingers shoot straight up. Notice how the fingers no longer touch the thumb. Our upstairs brain can't help us control our emotions, and now our feelings control us until we can back down the lid.

- **Green:** "My brain is good to go; I can listen, participate, and learn."
  Hand sign: gentle fist with fingers over the thumb.

- **Yellow:** "Caution/slow down; I am unsure how I feel; I may need help."

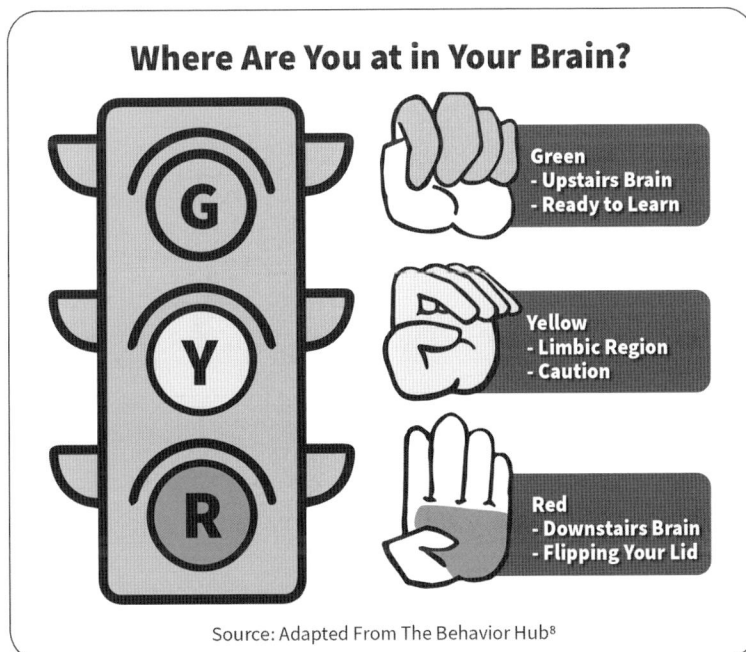

Where Are You at in Your Brain?

Green
- Upstairs Brain
- Ready to Learn

Yellow
- Limbic Region
- Caution

Red
- Downstairs Brain
- Flipping Your Lid

Source: Adapted From The Behavior Hub[8]

Hand sign: The thumb is tucked with fingers horizontal and flat over the thumb.

- **Red:** "I feel dysregulated (sad, angry, frustrated, out of sorts, or something else). I need help." Hand sign: Fingers are vertical and extended, and the hand is open.

If a student expresses that they are "yellow," it is appropriate to briefly share with the entire group that it is ok to not always feel "green."

We create a safe space to feel whatever we feel in the group. You don't need to fix the "yellow" feeling; just acknowledge it. Implement a co-regulation strategy such as your warm presence to soothe the student(s) and let them know you "see" them. Validate their feelings and continue with the lesson.

If a student says "red," assess safety issues and check to see if the student can and would like to stay in the group (receiving your co-regulating presence through the lesson) or needs something more. Check to see if you can support and discuss the issue after the group so the student can stay in the group. If the student needs one-on-one support, refer them to someone in the building who can give that focused attention while the group continues, assuring safety for the student feeling "red." This will model what we do when someone is in red for all students. During scheduled group time, ensure there is always a backup person to help a student who feels "red" and cannot stay in the group. Be sure to follow up with the student feeling "red" after the group.

Explain the Group Format: Explain where and how often you will meet. Share the list of topics. Explain that, in each meeting, you will discuss one of the topics together, then read the Story and answer questions. Discuss the logistics of what they'll do while you are reading; they'll be eating (if it is a lunch group) or completing their Coloring Sheet. Explain that they'll have time to work in pairs for the Skill Practice portion and play a "Would You Rather?" game. Finally, explain that at the end of each session, they'll be asked to give a one-sentence overview of what they've learned and how they plan to practice that lesson topic throughout the week.

Review Group Expectations: Print a copy of the Group Expectations. Review the expectations together with the students and answer questions as they arise. Collaborate with your group to determine whether you need to modify or add expectations.

Group Conclusion: Ask each student to summarize the information they learned from this session into one sentence. Students may share with their partners or the group.

Note to Facilitators: You can customize the material to fit the needs of your group. If your students are not yet readers, you can read the "Would You Rather?" game questions aloud and request that students move to different sides of the room to show their answers. If you're working with reticent students, they can write their responses to questions instead of sharing them aloud or break into smaller teams to discuss. Some facilitators may incorporate traditional games into the lessons if they have longer session times. Remember, the workbook is just the framework, but you will bring it to life!

MY UPSTAIRS AND DOWNSTAIRS BRAIN

MIND MAP

On the board, draw a mind map and ask students to consider the meaning of *emotion*.

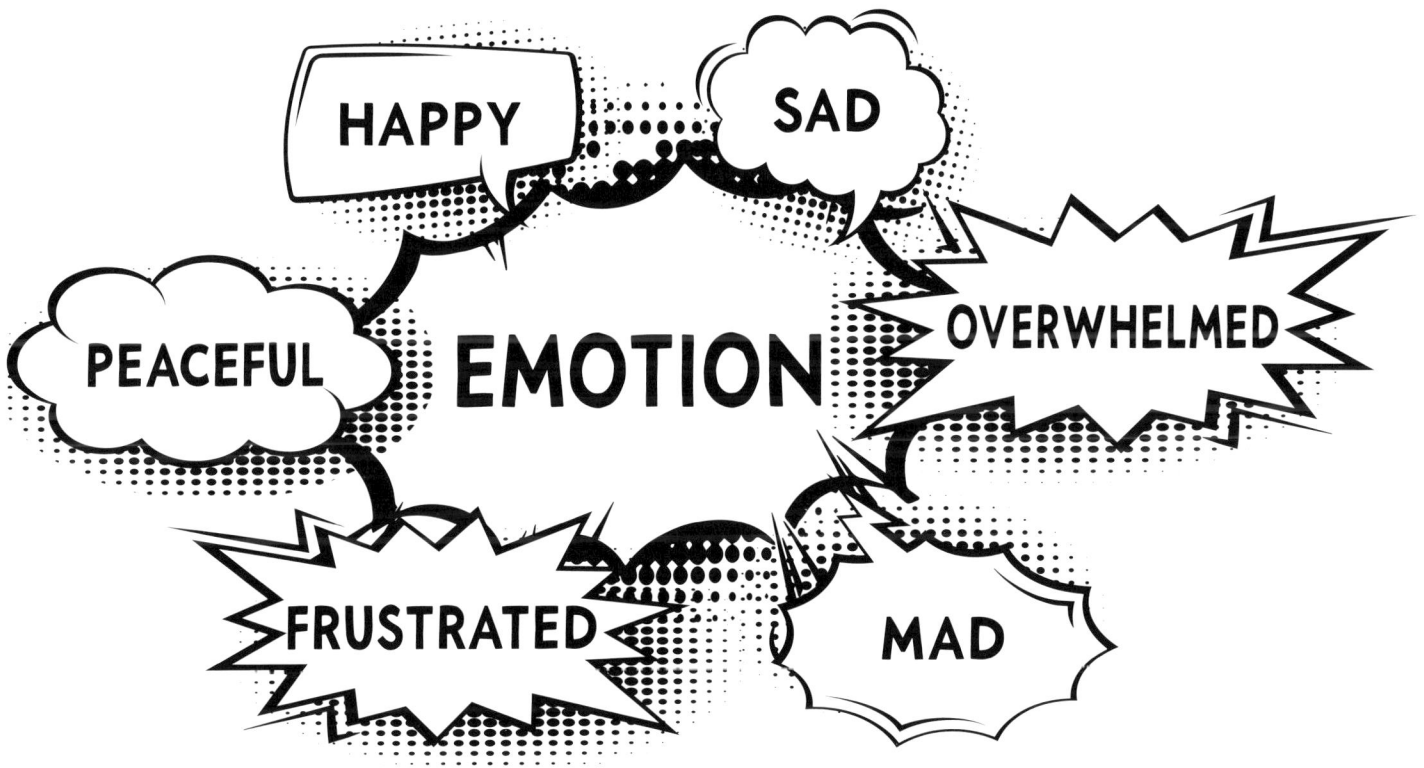

HAPPY

SAD

PEACEFUL

EMOTION

OVERWHELMED

FRUSTRATED

MAD

ASCA® STANDARDS

- **B-LS 4.** Self-motivation and self-direction for learning
- **B-SMS 2.** Self-discipline and self-control
- **B-SMS 10.** Ability to manage transitions and adapt to change
- **B-SS 4.** Empathy

In a small group format, complete the "brain stoplight check-in," which will be used each week to discuss whether they are in their upstairs or downstairs brain or somewhere in the middle. Point to the brain stoplight graphic for visual support. The following is a review; for a more in-depth explanation, please see the introductory lesson.

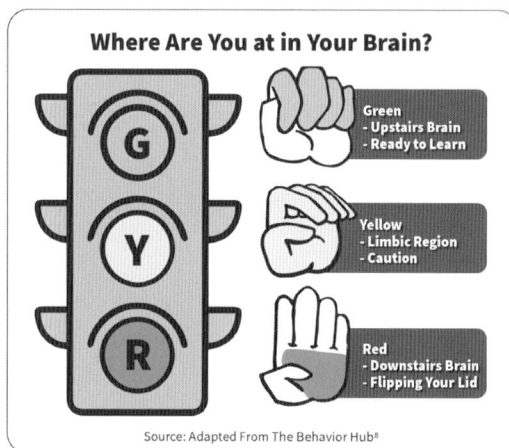

Where Are You at in Your Brain?

Green
- Upstairs Brain
- Ready to Learn

Yellow
- Limbic Region
- Caution

Red
- Downstairs Brain
- Flipping Your Lid

Source: Adapted From The Behavior Hub®

- **Green:** "My brain is good to go; I can listen, participate, and learn." (I am in my upstairs brain). Hand sign: gentle fist with fingers over the thumb

- **Yellow:** "Caution/slow down; I am unsure how I feel; I may need help." (I may be moving from my upstairs to my downstairs brain.) Hand sign: The thumb is tucked with fingers horizontal and flat over the thumb.

- **Red:** "I feel dysregulated (sad, angry, frustrated, out of sorts or something else). I need help" (I am in my downstairs brain). Hand sign: Fingers are vertical and extended, and the hand is open.

If a student expresses that they are "yellow," it is appropriate to briefly discuss with the group that we won't always feel "green." That's okay. Sometimes, we just need to feel what we feel without fixing it! Your attuned presence will be soothing for "yellow" feelings. Validate their feelings and continue with the lesson.

If the student says "red," assess safety issues and check to see if the student can and would like to stay in the group (receiving your co-regulating presence through the lesson) or needs something more active and supported. Check to see if you can support and discuss the issue after the group so the student can stay in the group. If the student needs one-on-one support, refer them to someone in the building who can give that focused attention while the group continues, assuring safety for the student feeling "red." Be sure to follow up with the student feeling "red" after the group.

Review the Group Expectations before reviewing the Mind Map. Then, read the Lesson Introduction and ask the Circle Time Questions before reading the Story and the Discussion Questions. Students can work in pairs to craft their responses or share with the whole group. Complete the Skill Practice, "Would You Rather?" game, and Additional Activities as time allows. Be sure to complete the Closing Considerations with each lesson.

We can learn to manage our big emotions by recognizing how we feel and by noticing sensations. That ability is located in our upstairs brain. The top or upstairs part of our brain helps us handle challenges and overwhelming feelings. When we feel unsafe and out of control, we are in our downstairs brain or the bottom part of our brain.

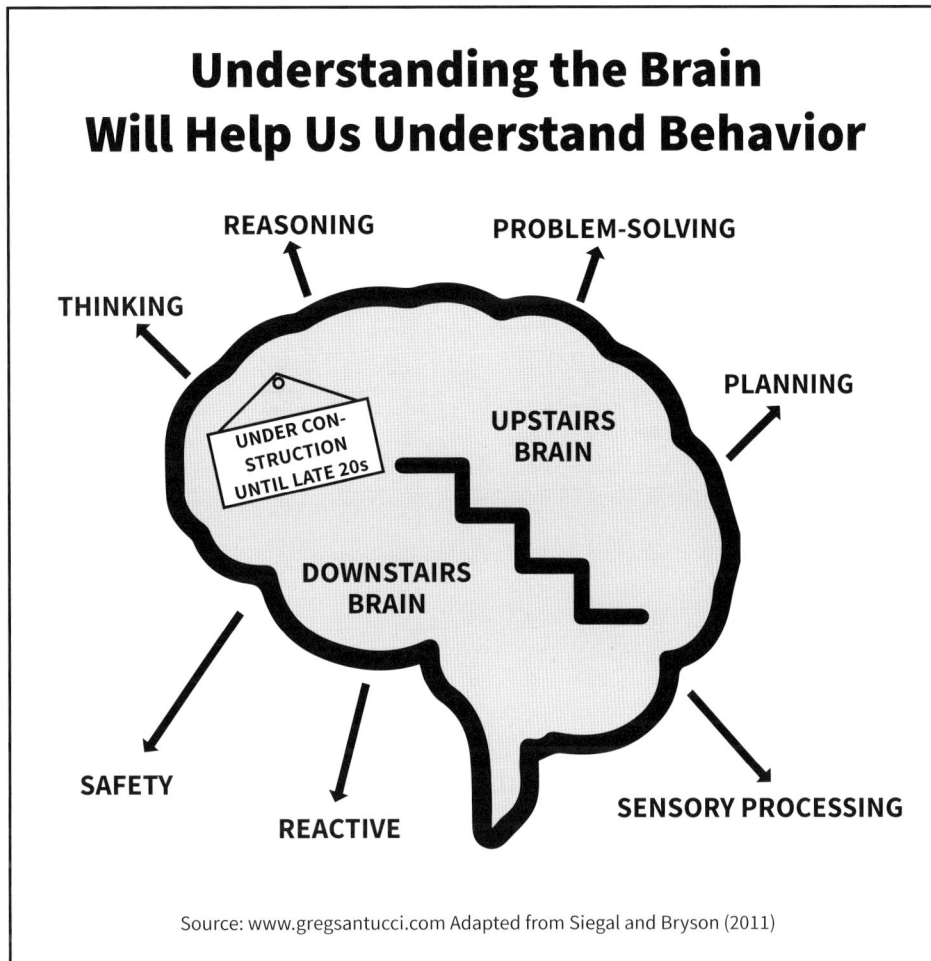

Understanding the Brain
Will Help Us Understand Behavior

REASONING

PROBLEM-SOLVING

THINKING

PLANNING

UNDER CON-
STRUCTION
UNTIL LATE 20s

UPSTAIRS
BRAIN

DOWNSTAIRS
BRAIN

SAFETY

REACTIVE

SENSORY PROCESSING

Source: www.gregsantucci.com Adapted from Siegal and Bryson (2011)

CIRCLE TIME QUESTIONS

Ask students to reflect and share their answers to the following questions with the group. Larger groups may need to be broken into smaller groups to give students ample time to share their answers and deepen the conversation.

- Have you ever felt "in the zone" or in your upstairs brain where you were happy and could do your best? If you feel comfortable, share with the group (speak, draw, or act it out, if time allows).

- Can you think of a time when you were in your downstairs brain and you "flipped your lid?"

- Everyone flips their lid (quickly going from upstairs to downstairs). Can you think of ways in which you were able to get your lid back down after it was flipped and move back to your upstairs brain?

Hand out coloring sheets and crayons or markers to younger students while the facilitator reads the story, if desired.

I Can Manage My Feelings

Chaos erupted in Ms. Mallory's classroom. Instead of the usual chatter, there were wide eyes and a few anxious whispers. Ms. Mallory had announced a fire drill, but not everyone was happy about it!

Olivia, usually the class chatterbox, was visibly nervous and began to cry. Matthew, unsure what to do about Olivia's crying, bolted out of the room.

Ms. Mallory stayed calm. She turned on soothing music, and everyone grabbed their spelling lists for a quick practice...everyone except Olivia. Ms. Mallory asked Jessie, Olivia's best friend, to sit with Olivia while Ms. Mallory went to find Matthew.

"Hey," Jessie whispered, concerned. "What's wrong?"

Olivia's voice trembled. "Remember when my mom burned dinner, and the fire alarm went off? LOUDEST, SCARIEST, SOUND EVER! I don't wanna hear it again!"

Jessie said, "Maybe you can wear headphones during the drill? They can give you noise-canceling superpowers!"

Olivia's face lit up. "Headphones! That's brilliant!"

Ms. Mallory returned with Matthew. "Sometimes," she explained, "when we're scared, our brains get stuck downstairs, all panicky. But we can take a deep breath, hold it for a couple of seconds, slowly let it out, ask for help, and use our upstairs brains to think clearly and figure out what to do next."

Suddenly, fire drills didn't seem so scary anymore. Olivia could wear her headphones, and Matthew learned a new way to settle his downstairs brain. Having tips for managing big, scary feelings made everything seem easier to handle.

- How do we know that Ms. Mallory was in her upstairs brain?
- How do we know that Jessie was in her upstairs brain?
- Why did Matthew run out of the room?
- Did Olivia and Mathew do anything wrong?
- Do you think Ms. Mallory and Jessie are always in their upstairs brains?
- If you were in the room, what do you think you would have done?

SKILL PRACTICE

Using the round-robin method, go around the table and ask students how they would practice each skill, giving everyone a chance to answer one question. You can adapt Skill Practice to allow students to respond in pairs or write their answers on paper.

- Identify where the upstairs brain is on the hand.

- Identify where the downstairs brain is on the hand.

- What does the hand look like when you feel peaceful and creative?

- What does the hand look like when you feel overwhelmed and distracted?

- Give an example of an upstairs brain moment and show using the hand model.

- Give an example of a downstairs brain moment and show using the hand model.

- Share why learning the hand-brain model is helpful with managing big emotions.

ADDITIONAL ACTIVITIES

- Have students act out different versions of downstairs brain moments. Ask students how to shift the downstairs brain moment into an upstairs brain moment by asking, "What could you do instead?" (Examples could be: failing a test, falling hard off their skateboard, forgetting to prepare for a performance, or losing their favorite t-shirt.)

- Have students take turns acting out the following big emotional moments while pretending they are robots. Ask them why this is extra challenging.

  - Finding their puppy after it was lost.

  - Seeing someone bullying your best friend.

  - Discovering a treasure chest full of gold.

  - Hearing that someone said something mean about you behind your back.

CLOSING CONSIDERATIONS

Downstairs brain moments are normal! We aren't meant to be robots. Feelings are just feelings; they aren't good or bad. They are there for a reason. We can regain balance and control. We often need help to do this, so it's important not to feel bad when things seem too hard to solve on our own.

Ask students to summarize the content of this session's lesson in one sentence.

Ask students to recognize both upstairs brain and downstairs brain moments in themselves and others this week. Then, encourage them to notice what helps others and themselves get back into balance and go back upstairs when they are downstairs.

Playing the "Would You Rather?" game is a fun and engaging activity for students to develop their critical thinking skills. Students will reflect on their experience, evaluate their options based on their preferences, and reflect on the opinions of others, providing a different perspective and strengthening their sense of connection to one another.

WOULD YOU RATHER?

Copy and cut out the questions for small groups to discuss, or have each person stand in the center of the room and move towards one side or the other to show their vote for either option as the facilitator reads the questions aloud.

WOULD YOU RATHER ASK FOR HELP WHEN YOU ENCOUNTER A PROBLEM OR TRY SOMETHING YOURSELF FIRST?

WOULD YOU RATHER ALWAYS BE IN YOUR UPSTAIRS BRAIN OR BE ABLE TO HELP SOMEONE STUCK IN THEIR DOWNSTAIRS BRAIN?

WOULD YOU RATHER GO THROUGH LIFE WITHOUT PROBLEMS OR LEARN AND GROW FROM YOUR TRIALS?

WOULD YOU RATHER BE A ROBOT WHO NEVER MESSES UP OR BE A PERSON WHO MAKES MISTAKES THAT CAN BE FIXED?

WOULD YOU RATHER FIGURE OUT HOW TO HELP A FRIEND IN THEIR DOWNSTAIRS BRAIN OR HOPE SOMEONE ELSE HELPS THEM?

WOULD YOU RATHER IGNORE UNCOMFORTABLE FEELINGS INSIDE YOU, HOPING THEY GO AWAY OR TALK TO SOMEONE ABOUT THEM?

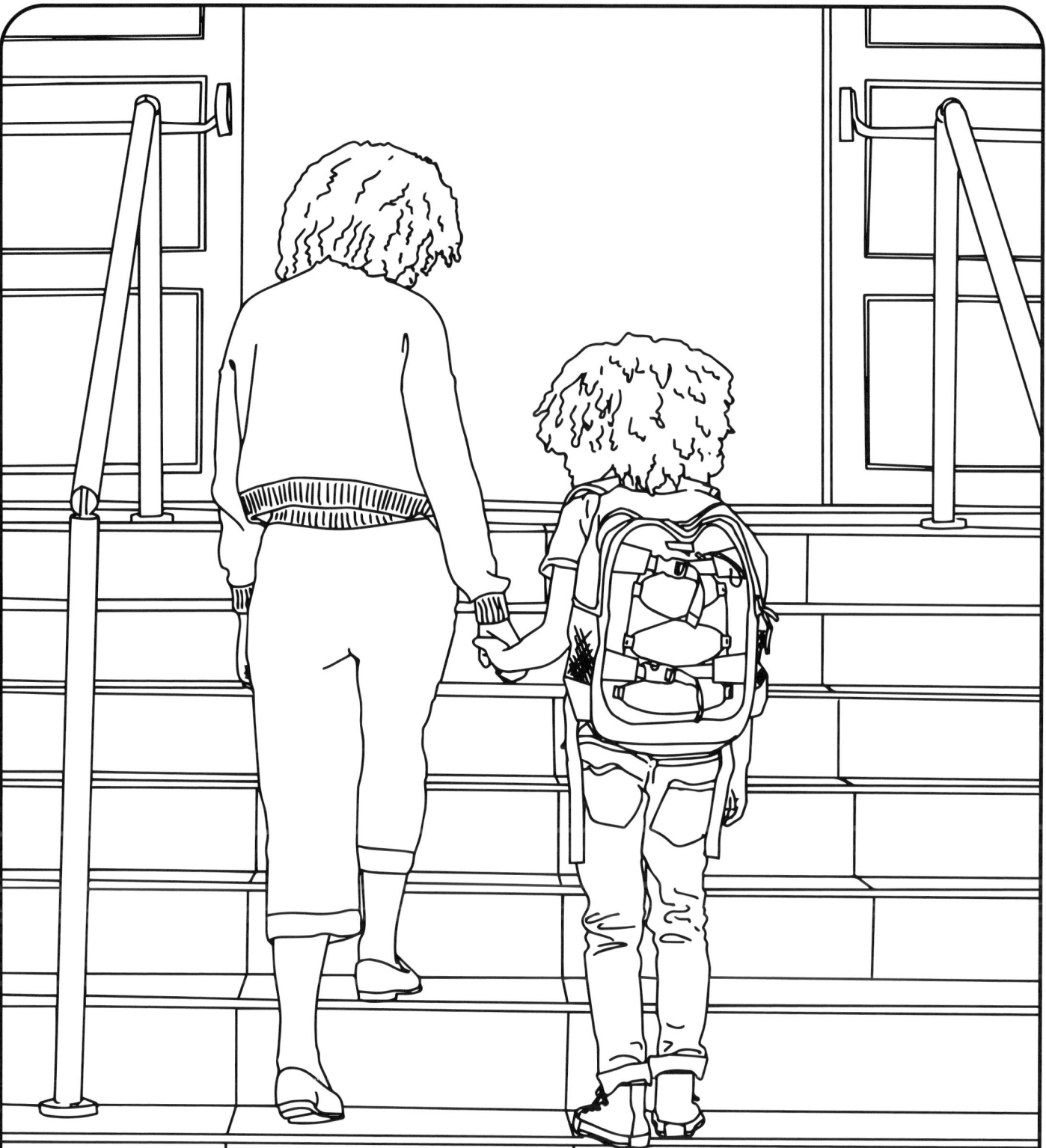

We all have downstairs brain moments!
We can ask for help and avoid getting
stuck downstairs.

CHAPTER 2

SENSING MY SENSES

MIND MAP

On the board, draw a mind map and ask students to consider the meaning of *senses*.

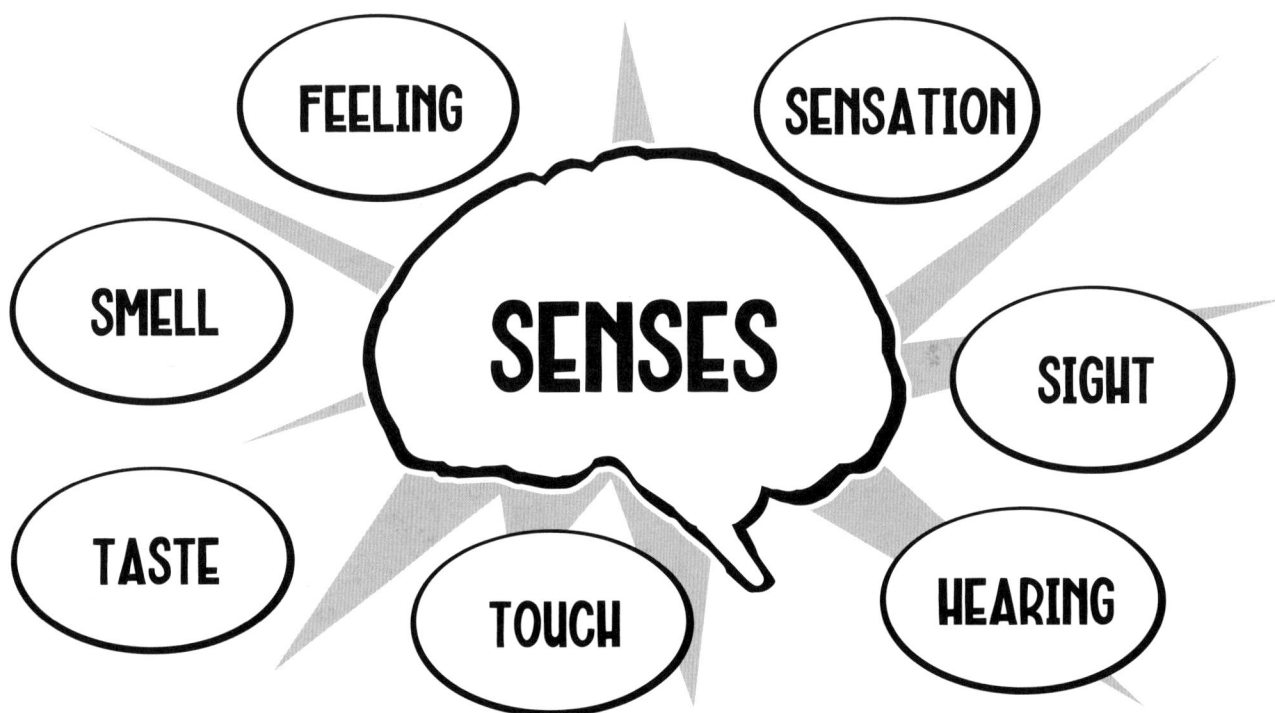

ASCA® STANDARDS

- **B-LS 2.** Creative approach to learning, tasks, and problem-solving
- **B-SMS 4.** Delayed gratification for long-term rewards
- **B-SMS 7.** Effective coping skills
- **B-SS 8.** Advocacy skills for self and others and ability to assert self, when necessary

In a small group format, complete a brief check-in with students by asking them to indicate their feelings using the brain stoplight check-in.

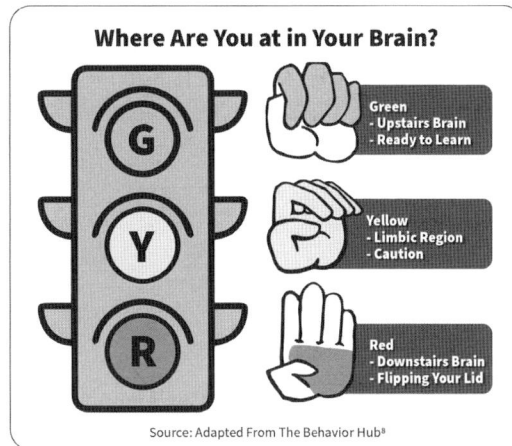

Where Are You at in Your Brain?

Green
- Upstairs Brain
- Ready to Learn

Yellow
- Limbic Region
- Caution

Red
- Downstairs Brain
- Flipping Your Lid

Source: Adapted From The Behavior Hub®

Review the Group Expectations before asking students to share their knowledge of the topic from the previous week. Ask students to share one thing they did differently this week because of what they learned in last week's lesson. Together, review the Mind Map. Then, read the Lesson Introduction and ask the Circle Time Questions before reading the Story and asking the Discussion Questions. Students can work in pairs to craft their responses or share with the whole group. Complete the Skill Practice, "Would You Rather?" game, and Additional Activities as time allows. Be sure to complete the Closing Considerations with each lesson.

LESSON INTRODUCTION

We need our senses. They help us enjoy life. Sometimes, our senses get overwhelmed and overstimulated, leading us to flip our lids. By becoming more aware of and understanding what our senses are trying to tell us, we can learn from those moments and get better at getting our lids back down and shifting to our upstairs brain.

Raise your left hand for yes and right hand for no.

Have you ever had downstairs brain moments with:

- Sounds: Are some sounds too loud or jarring, or do you hate it when it's too quiet?
- Smells: Are some too strong and make you sneeze or want to run away?
- Touches and feels: Are some textures itchy, bumpy, slippery, or irritating?
- Tastes: Are some too strong or have a weird texture?
- Sight: Are some lights too bright or distracting?
- Temperature: Do you get too hot or too cold?
- Balance: Do you get lightheaded, heavy, or disconnected?
- Do you ever feel overly tired and unable to concentrate?
- Have you ever felt overly energetic like you can't slow down?

We will explore what your senses are trying to tell you, how we can prevent your lid from flipping, and how to get the lid back down when it flips.

Ask students to reflect and share their answers to the following questions with the group. Larger groups may need to be broken into smaller groups to give students ample time to share their answers and deepen the conversation.

- What ways of reducing distracting noises help you most?

- Which works better for you? Talking, drawing, or writing about it?

- What types of movements settle your senses? Jumping, climbing, swinging, rocking, bumping into things in safe, fun ways?

STORY TIME

Hand out the crossword puzzle for students to work on while the facilitator reads the story, if desired. (Answer Key on page 91.)

Sam's Senses

Sam was struggling at school. His teacher noticed he had difficulty staying in his chair and completing work. Sometimes, he would even fall off his chair during lessons.

"Sam, can you tell me what's happening inside you when you fall out of your chair?" Ms. Morris kneeled next to him. Sam looked embarrassed and had a hard time looking at her. "Am I in trouble?"

"No, not at all! I am just worried about you!" She put a gentle hand on his shoulder, and he flinched. "Oh, I am sorry, Sam." She said, "I forgot you don't like to be touched. I will respect that."

"It's because I get itchy, and it feels hot when people touch me," Sam replied.

"Ahhh, this is important information. It makes me wonder if sitting in your chair gets uncomfortable, like when people touch you," she ventured.

Sam replied, "When I am in my chair, I get anxious trying to sit still. Sometimes I get dizzy."

Ms. Morris looked concerned. "That must feel very disconcerting, and I can see how it could lead to you falling out of your seat!"

"Especially when it gets noisy, I just want to escape it," Sam stated emphatically.

"Mmm, I bet." Ms. Morris offered, "Sometimes when I feel overwhelmed, I want to escape too!"

She paused and thought, "Sam, have you ever tried headphones? I wonder if you would like to try that when you need a break from the noise in the room."

He nodded, and she continued, "We still need to find a solution to your falling from your chair. We don't want you to get hurt. Maybe we need a team meeting to ensure we meet your needs and that there isn't something I am missing here. In the meantime, if you feel dizzy, please let me know."

During afternoon math, Ms. Morris looked at Sam and noticed he was agitated. He started leaning on his desk and sliding onto the floor. She asked him, "Sam, do you want to sit on the ground instead of your chair?" He brightened, "Sure!"

Soon, he was lying on his stomach. When she checked on him after the lesson, she saw that he had completed his assignment and had started a new one—remarkable! He seemed happier, too; he was so proud of himself.

After that, he was given a choice every day of how and where he wanted to sit, and, most days, he chose the quiet corner facing the wall and lying on his stomach. He was content and productive. It was a simple change that made a huge difference.

DISCUSSION QUESTIONS

- How do we know that Sam was struggling?

- How were Sam's senses getting in the way of helping him stay on task?

- What were Sam's senses communicating?

- What other ideas do you have that could help Sam or other students who struggle with overwhelmed senses?

SKILL PRACTICE

Using the round-robin method, go around the table and ask students how they would practice each skill, giving every student a chance to answer one question. Skill practice can be adapted to allow students to respond in pairs or write their answers on scratch paper.

If you felt overwhelmed, how would you adjust or accommodate your environment to soothe your senses if:

- Someone was watching tv loudly in the room you were in?

- All the lights were on in the house?

- A skunk had sprayed in your yard?

- The tag on your shirt is rubbing the back of your neck?

- Your sandwich is soggy?

- You feel confused and can't think of answers?

- You feel hungry and distracted?

- You feel shivery and cold?

- You feel uncomfortable in your clothes?

- You are having a hard time hearing directions?

ADDITIONAL ACTIVITIES

- Tell students that breaks can prevent downstairs brain moments! Have them sit quietly with soft eyes and listen to you as you help them scan every part of their body, noticing whether they need a break. "Go inside yourself and listen to your body. What is each part telling you? Start with your head and move down to your toes. Notice any sensations. When you notice something pause, figure out what it is communicating. A growling stomach asks for food, and a full bladder asks for a bathroom break. Restless legs need movement. A foggy memory requires a brain game and movement."

- Direct students to listen as you read a list of things that can indicate we might be about to become dysregulated and move into the downstairs brain and give a thumbs-up if any of these sound familiar to them being precursors for their dysregulation:

  - Wanting to run away and not talk to anyone

  - Wanting to do my own thing; sick of being told what to do

  - Skin feels warm and sweaty

  - Feeling pressured

  - Can't figure out what to do next

  - Feeling out of control

  - Feeling exhausted

  - Feeling itchy and irritable

CLOSING CONSIDERATIONS

When we remove roadblocks, the best method for solving problems becomes clearer. Often, that means we must slow down and pay attention to what we see, hear, smell, and feel. Our senses can give us a wealth of information, and accommodating our sensory needs will soothe and help us feel better.

Ask students to summarize the content of this session's lesson in one sentence.

Ask students to consider a recent time when their senses were overwhelmed. What was the emotion communicating? Encourage them to be intentional this week about noticing what is getting in the way of them being able to solve their problems. In pairs or groups of three, students may share their answers. If time allows, a few students may share with the whole group.

Playing the "Would You Rather?" game is a fun and engaging activity for students to develop their critical thinking skills. Students will reflect on their experience, evaluate their options based on their preferences, and reflect on the opinions of others, providing a different perspective and strengthening their sense of connection to one another.

WOULD YOU RATHER?

Copy and cut out the questions for small groups to discuss, or have each person stand in the center of the room and move towards one side or the other to show their vote for either option as the facilitator reads the questions aloud.

WOULD YOU RATHER MUNCH ON SOMETHING SOUR OR SWEET?

WOULD YOU RATHER SIT ON A WOBBLE SEAT/ BOUNCY BALL OR SIT OR LAY ON THE FLOOR?

WOULD YOU RATHER SMELL SOMETHING FRUITY OR SOMETHING WOODSY?

WOULD YOU RATHER WEAR SOME SUNGLASSES OR HAVE THE LIGHTS TURNED DIM?

WOULD YOU RATHER WEAR HEADPHONES OR WORK IN A QUIET AREA?

WOULD YOU RATHER LISTEN TO LOUDER, UPBEAT, OR QUIET, SLOWER MUSIC?

SENSATIONAL SENSES

```
B  S  M  Z  M  Y  D  S  A  N  S  G  B  Y  F
A  O  E  I  Y  R  D  O  T  O  A  I  H  L  F
Q  U  T  A  D  U  T  N  O  I  T  D  E  K  E
S  R  M  O  O  Q  U  I  E  T  C  L  A  R  E
J  W  H  L  H  N  M  A  E  S  I  K  V  A  L
I  A  E  T  H  G  I  R  B  G  J  A  Y  P  I
X  S  R  E  O  I  T  Y  H  C  T  I  Y  S  N
Z  I  F  R  T  O  T  U  N  S  L  Z  M  G
B  G  M  W  I  G  M  Z  Y  V  K  T  K  C  Y
B  U  M  P  Y  N  J  S  T  C  F  O  S  R  Q
R  J  D  T  L  R  G  F  I  Y  V  R  O  E  U
S  A  L  T  Y  Y  X  R  U  U  H  V  D  C  Z
Z  Q  O  D  Z  Q  P  N  R  Q  A  K  K  J  S
V  J  C  M  K  Y  V  C  F  S  I  Y  I  L  E
J  N  O  I  T  A  S  N  E  S  T  I  N  K  Y
```

Salty	Quiet	Stinky
Sweet	Jarring	Sticky
Sour	Heavy	Feeling
Bitter	Light	Sensation
Bright	Itchy	Hot
Dim	Smooth	Cold
Sparkly	Fruity	Prickly
Loud	Savory	Bumpy

Self-Compassion

MIND MAP

On the board, draw a mind map and ask students to consider the meaning of *self-compassion*.

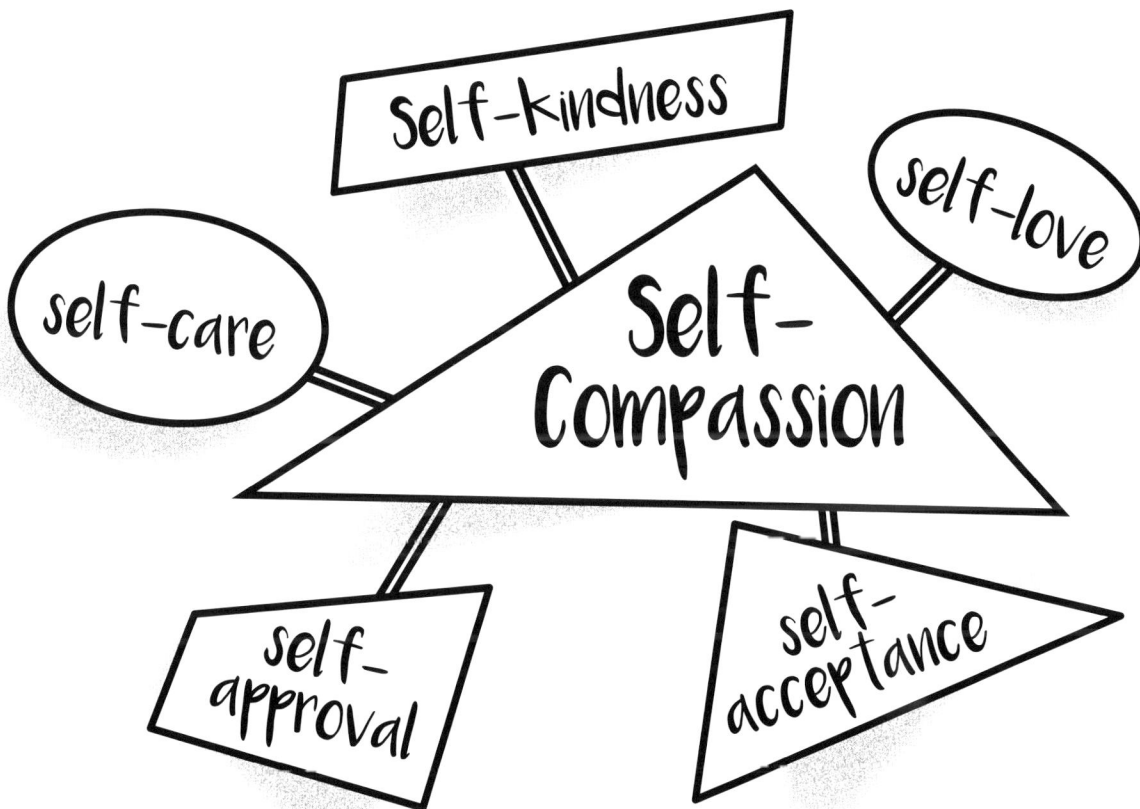

ASCA® STANDARDS

- **B-LS 4.** Self-motivation and self-direction for learning
- **B-SMS 1.** Responsibility for self and actions
- **B-SMS 8.** Balance of school, home, and community activities
- **B-SS 8.** Advocacy Skills for self and others and ability to assert self, when necessary

In a small group format, complete a brief check-in with students by asking them to indicate their feelings using the brain stoplight check-in.

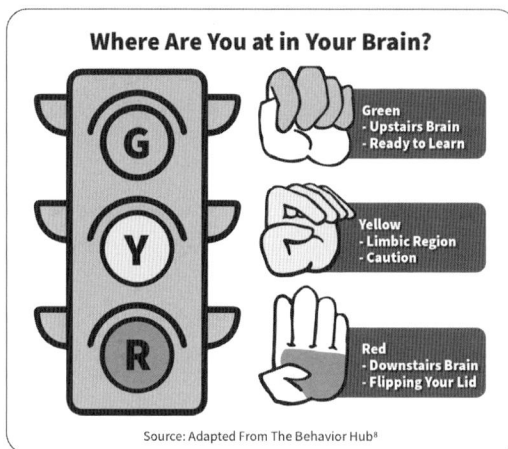

Where Are You at in Your Brain?

Green
- Upstairs Brain
- Ready to Learn

Yellow
- Limbic Region
- Caution

Red
- Downstairs Brain
- Flipping Your Lid

Source: Adapted From The Behavior Hub®

Review the Group Expectations before asking students to share their knowledge of the topic from the previous week. Ask students to share one thing they did differently this week because of what they learned in last week's lesson. Together, review the Mind Map. Then, read the Lesson Introduction and ask the Circle Time Questions before reading the Story and asking the Discussion Questions. Students can work in pairs to craft their responses or share with the whole group. Complete the Skill Practice, "Would You Rather?" game, and Additional Activities as time allows. Be sure to complete the Closing Considerations with each lesson.

LESSON INTRODUCTION

Introduce the subject for the week by defining Self-Compassion

Self-compassion: Feeling kindness toward ourselves leads us to help ourselves.

We often spend a lot of time discussing how to help others. Did you know that we can and should care about ourselves and meet our needs as well? When we are compassionate toward ourselves, we can help others better. When our own needs are met, we become stronger and more capable of meeting other's needs.

Think of a car. Can the vehicle drive if there is no gas in the tank? Think of the gas as self-compassion. We need "gas" in our tanks to go far, so we need to fill up on kindness and caring for ourselves to do what we need to do.

Sometimes, it's hard to care for ourselves because we feel that our needs don't matter, or we may feel that we are unworthy. The reality is that everybody messes up and makes mistakes. We are all human, and self-compassion allows us to forgive ourselves and try again!

Ask students to reflect and share their answers to the following questions with the group. Larger groups may need to be broken into smaller groups to give students ample time to share their answers and deepen the conversation.

- Have you ever felt burned out, like you have nothing left to give and your "gas tank" is empty? What does that feel like?

- Why do you think it is often harder to have compassion for ourselves than others?

- Do you think there is a difference between selfishness and self-compassion? Explain!

STORY TIME

Hand out coloring sheets and crayons or markers to younger students while the facilitator reads the story, if desired.

Savvy Says No

"Savvy, I need your help!" Miss Wilson called from the front of the classroom. Savvy didn't even think she could say no to that request! But if she was honest with herself, she felt like she had heard that all day from her friends, family, and teachers.

She loved helping out; it was one of her best strengths. However, she started noticing that she was falling behind on homework and chores because she was putting everyone's requests ahead of her own.

"I really don't know what to do," she told herself. She decided it was a problem she just couldn't solve now and helped Miss Wilson pass out papers instead of reading the assigned chapter.

But that night, after dinner, Savvy's mom asked her to do the dishes, and Savvy broke down in tears.

This caught her mom off guard, "I didn't think dishes were such a big deal!"

"It's just that I am so far behind on homework, and I hoped to get caught up tonight. I guess doing dishes instead made me think I will never get caught up." Savvy sobbed.

"Oh, sweetie, I didn't mean to overwhelm you, I can see how hard it is for you to balance your own needs against helping out." She hugged Savvy and asked, "Can I teach you something that has helped me out?"

"You need help?" Savvy was surprised.

Her mom laughed, "Oh yes, I have a hard time saying no as well, so I have learned a few phrases that make it easier, and I want to share them with you."

They sat down, and Savvy's mom gave her a list of ideas on what to say when she became overwhelmed and felt like she couldn't help.

- "I can help you later!"

- "Let me help next time!"

- "I want to help, but I need to do my own chores and homework first."

- "Unfortunately, I can't right now."

- "I'm honored you asked me, but no."

- "No."

- "I need help with that."

Savvy's mom looked her in the eyes, "You are important. Your own needs matter. You aren't being selfish when you take time for yourself."

"Thanks, Mom, I needed to hear that!" Savvy winked at her mom and they finished the dishes together.

DISCUSSION QUESTIONS

- How do we know that Savvy struggled with self-compassion?

- How did Savvy learn to meet her needs and stay true to herself?

- How can you speak up for yourself so people don't overlook your needs?

- Is it possible to meet your own needs and help others? Give an example.

- Do you think it will be easy for Savvy to be compassionate to herself from now own? Why or why not?

SKILL PRACTICE

Using the round-robin method, go around the table and ask students how they would practice self-compassion, giving every student a chance to answer one question. Skill practice can be adapted to allow students to answer in pairs or write their answers on scratch paper.

How would you practice self-compassion if:

- You were exhausted but still had several things you wanted to accomplish that day?

- You failed a test?

- You forgot to do something you promised your parents you would do?

- You slept through your alarm?

- You decided not to try out for the school play because you were too scared?

- You told your friend you were not able to help them because you had too many things to do that day?

- You promised someone you would help them but woke up sick?

- Your classmate keeps asking you if they can look at your answers?

- Your teacher tells you they think you can do better?

- You know you could study harder, but you also want to help your sister?

ADDITIONAL ACTIVITIES

- Direct students to write the following sayings on scrap paper and tape them where they can see them. Encourage them to repeat each and let them know that they may not fully believe or feel the truthfulness of each statement but saying it aloud will get them on the path to it becoming true to them!

  - I matter!

  - I am enough!

  - I am worthy!

  - I don't have to be perfect!

  - I am strong!

  - I can show myself compassion.

- Direct students to imagine being an undercover detective who interviewed several of their family and friends, asking, "What is (name of student) good at? What are their strengths, skills, and capabilities? What do you like about them?" Have the students share the findings of the investigation with the class. "They described my strengths and skills as..."

CLOSING CONSIDERATIONS

Sometimes, we treat others better than we treat ourselves! When we care for ourselves by asking for help or taking time to meet our needs, we will be stronger and more able to accomplish what we need to do and help others. Just like phones need to be charged, so do your internal batteries!

Ask students to summarize the content of this session's lesson in one sentence.

Ask students to consider ways to charge their own batteries and be kind to themselves. Encourage them to consider what they have been doing that works and what they could do better throughout the week. Students may share their answers in pairs or groups of three. If time allows, a few students may share with the whole group.

Playing the "Would You Rather?" game is a fun and engaging activity for students to develop their critical thinking skills. Students will reflect on their experience, evaluate their options based on their preferences, and reflect on the opinions of others, providing a different perspective and strengthening their sense of connection to one another.

Would you Rather?

Copy and cut out the questions for small groups to discuss, or have each person stand in the center of the room and move towards one side or the other to show their vote for either option as the facilitator reads the questions aloud.

WOULD YOU RATHER HELP YOURSELF OR SOMEONE ELSE?

WOULD YOU RATHER ASK FOR HELP OR MEET YOUR OWN NEEDS WITHOUT HELP?

WOULD YOU RATHER TRY SOMETHING NEW OR USE A STRATEGY YOU KNOW WILL WORK?

WOULD YOU RATHER SAY KIND WORDS TO YOURSELF OR SOMEONE ELSE?

WOULD YOU RATHER TAKE A BREAK WHEN YOU ARE TIRED OR PUSH THROUGH?

WOULD YOU RATHER WRITE A LIST OF YOUR STRENGTHS OR SHARE THEM OUT LOUD?

I AM OUTTA THIS WORLD!

What are your cosmic talents that help you reach for the stars?

_____
_____
_____
_____
_____
_____

What interSTELLAR powers do you possess that help you soar and shine bright?

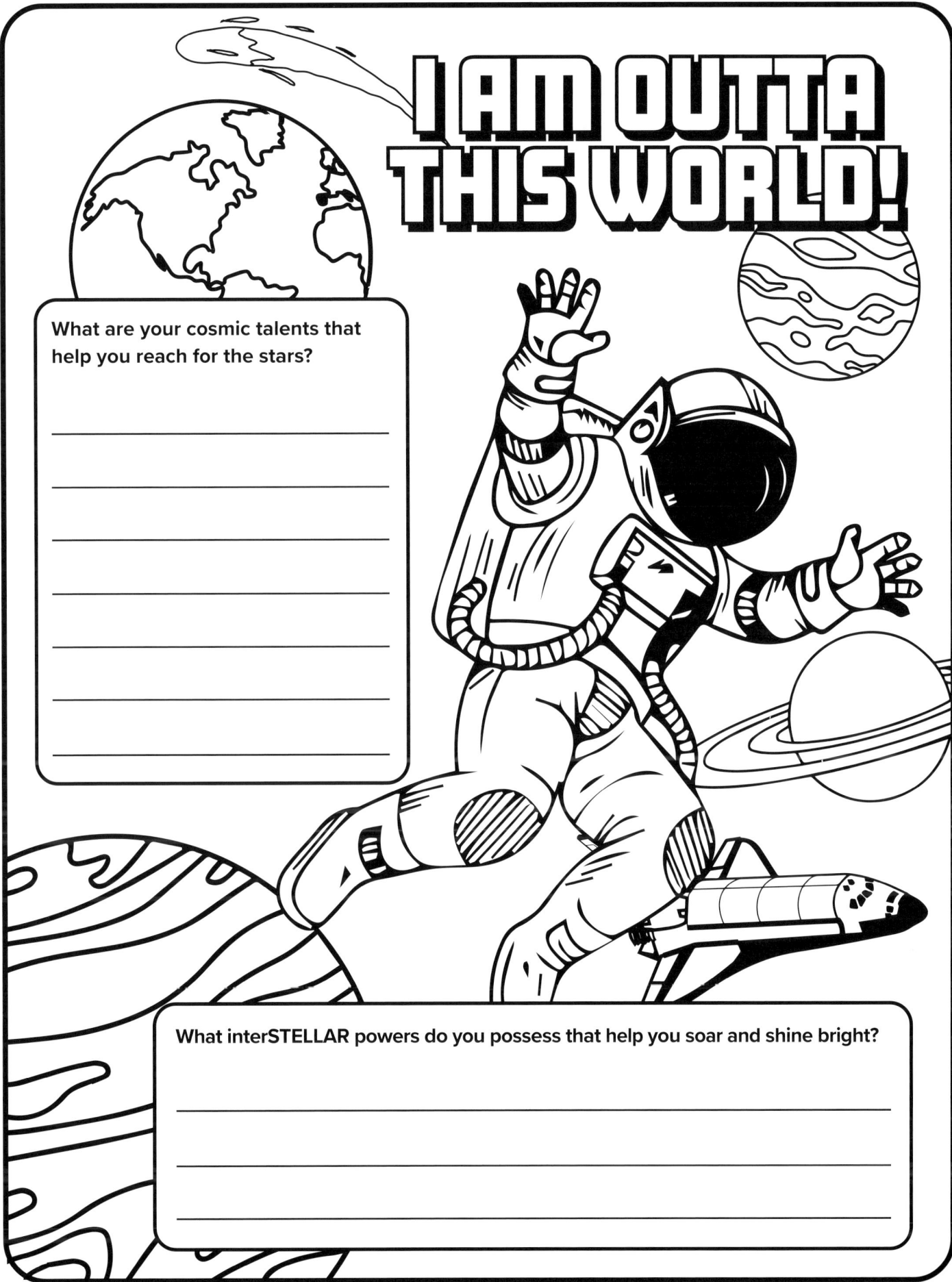

_____
_____
_____

Safe and Positive Relationships

MIND MAP

On the board, draw a mind map and ask students to consider the meaning of *relationship*.

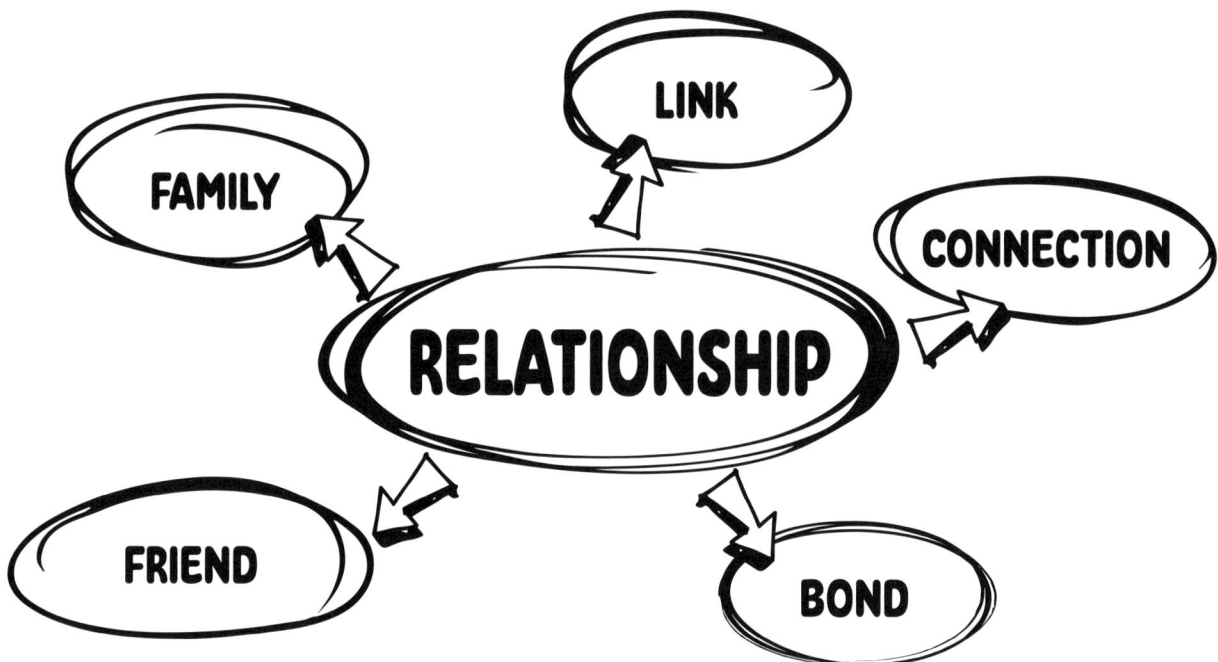

ASCA® STANDARDS

- **B-LS 9.** Decision-making, informed by gathering evidence, getting others' perspectives, and recognizing personal bias
- **B-SMS 9.** Personal Safety Skills
- **B-SS 2.** Positive, respectful, and supportive relationships with students who are similar to and different from them
- **B-SS 3.** Positive relationships with adults to support success

DIRECTIONS

In a small group format, complete a brief check-in with students by asking them to indicate their feelings using the brain stoplight check-in.

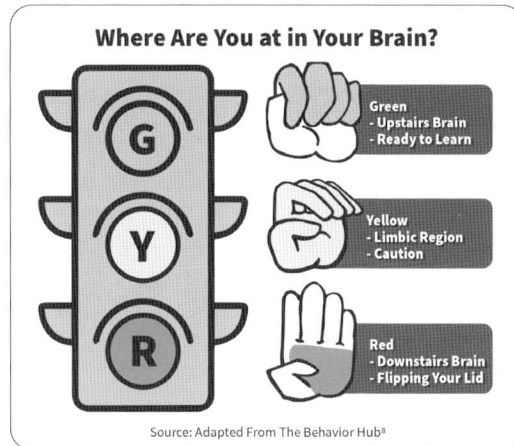

Where Are You at in Your Brain?

Green
- Upstairs Brain
- Ready to Learn

Yellow
- Limbic Region
- Caution

Red
- Downstairs Brain
- Flipping Your Lid

Source: Adapted From The Behavior Hub[8]

Review the Group Expectations before asking students to share their knowledge of the topic from the previous week. Ask students to share one thing they did differently this week because of what they learned in last week's lesson. Together, review the Mind Map. Then, read the Lesson Introduction and ask the Circle Time Questions before reading the Story and the Discussion Questions. Students can work in pairs to craft their responses or share with the whole group. Complete the Skill Practice, "Would You Rather?" Game and Additional Activities as time allows. Be sure to complete the Closing Considerations with each lesson.

LESSON INTRODUCTION

If we are dysregulated and in our downstairs best we can more easily become regulated and shift to our upstairs brain when someone helps comfort and soothe us, letting us know we are okay.

To access and use our upstairs brain, we need people who care about us. They help us feel safe and happy. When we feel safe and happy, it's easier to control our feelings. Safe and positive attachments are essential for our physical and emotional health. We aren't meant to do everything by ourselves. Friends, family, and other people can help us through tough times.

CIRCLE TIME QUESTIONS

Ask students to reflect and share their answers to the following questions with the group. Larger groups may need to be broken into smaller groups to give students ample time to share their answers and deepen the conversation.

- How do you know if someone is safe and positive and will help you?

- Describe what it feels like to have someone help you when you are struggling.

- Do you feel it is possible to ask for help when we are dysregulated or in your downstairs brain? Why or why not?

Hand out out coloring sheets and crayons or markers to younger students while the facilitator reads the story, if desired.

I Won't Let You Drift Away

It was a special day in Mr. Oliver's classroom! Someone from the aquarium was coming to share information on animals, and Gemma and Dallin absolutely could not wait. They were twins and did everything together.

When the biologist brought out the first animal, Gemma went pale. It was an octopus, and even though it fit in the palm of her hand, the tentacles seemed slimy and terrifying. She turned to Dallin and told him she didn't want to look anymore.

Dallin knew her fears were real, but he also knew she would feel sad to miss seeing the other animals. He told Gemma to close her eyes until the next animal came out, and he would keep talking to her and telling her everything that was happening. She asked him if he could hold her hand until she wasn't scared. When Dallin held her hand when she was nervous, it helped her heart stop racing.

Dallin smiled widely when the next animal came out and told Gemma to hurry and open her eyes! It was an adorable otter. Gemma was mesmerized as the biologist explained to the class that otters love to swim in groups because they are very social animals, and relationships are essential to their survival.

One of the most remarkable facts the biologist shared was that otters hold hands with each other while sleeping so they don't drift away. Otters also link together during storms to make floating over the waves easier! This is called "rafting."

"Dallin, we are otters!" she giggled, holding up their interlocked hands. "You are keeping me safe!!"

Dallin replied, "Too bad we aren't floating in a river with the otters right now. That would be the best!" They both laughed.

The biologist told the class that otters make sure no one gets lost or left behind, that staying close and relying on each other makes the otters stronger and more buoyant, and that otters need each other for their overall well-being. Dallin looked at Gemma and giggled.

Gemma knew that Dallin would keep her safe during life's storms, and she could do that for him, too. She gave Dallin a big hug. She felt grateful to have the best otter buddy in the whole world.

DISCUSSION QUESTIONS

- In what ways are humans like otters?

- How did Dallin help Gemma?

- What are ways someone has helped you feel better and and what are things you have done to help others feel better?

- What storms do you need an otter buddy for in your life?

- Who are your otter buddies?

SKILL PRACTICE

One of the hardest things to do when trying to help someone is knowing what to say and what not to say. It's okay to say, "I am not sure what to say, but I am here." Just sitting together or listening while they talk helps!

Sometimes, we try to help people but say too much and talk about ourselves. Saying "Me too!" validates someone's feelings, but we must be careful not to "hijack" the moment and focus on ourselves when we need to listen to the other person. Being a good listener makes you a good otter buddy to lean on, and when someone listens to us and we lean on them, it helps us feel better in return.

Read the following phrases (mix them up) and have students indicate phrases that help someone feel better with a thumbs-up and indicate phrases that would not help with a thumbs-down.

Thumbs-Up Phrases:

- You've got this.

- We can handle this.

- I'm right here if you need me.

- You are safe.

- I'm listening.

- I understand.

- Would you like a drink of water?

- Sometimes, I have hard times too.

- I won't leave you.

- I am going to ask someone to help us.

- You don't have to be sad on your own.

- I got scared too.

Thumbs-Down Phrases:

- Let me tell you what happened to me.

- You shouldn't feel scared. There is nothing to be afraid of.

- It's not that big of a deal.

- Calm down.

- If you would just listen this wouldn't happen.

- You made a mistake.

- It's not worth crying over.

- Big kids don't cry.

- Boys should act tough.

- There is no reason to be upset. I have had it worse.

ADDITIONAL ACTIVITIES

- Choose a friend or family member you want to express gratitude for and write them a thank you card describing how they have helped you feel better.

- List three ways you have been a good friend or family member by helping someone feel better when they struggled.

CLOSING CONSIDERATIONS

We need others to keep us safe and help us through difficult times. Asking for help is not a sign of weakness. Quite the opposite! It's a skill that can strengthen us and increase our ability to manage big emotions. Some people are emotionally and physically safe to be around, and this helps us feel better. Those people make great otter buddies. If someone doesn't keep you safe, ask for help from someone who does.

Ask students to summarize the content of this session's lesson in one sentence.

Ask students to consider how they will practice being an otter buddy throughout the week as both the giver and receiver of emotional safety. Students may share their answers in pairs or groups of three. If time allows, a few students may share with the whole group.

Playing the "Would You Rather?" game is a fun and engaging activity for students to develop their critical thinking skills. Students will reflect on their experience, evaluate their options based on their preferences, and reflect on the opinions of others, providing a different perspective and strengthening their sense of connection to one another.

Would You Rather?

Copy and cut out the questions for small groups to discuss, or have each person stand in the center of the room and move towards one side or the other to show their vote for either option as the facilitator reads the questions aloud.

WOULD YOU RATHER BE LEFT ALONE WHEN YOU ARE SCARED OR ASK FOR HELP?

WOULD YOU RATHER HAVE SOMEONE SIT NEXT TO YOU QUIETLY WHEN YOU ARE IN YOUR DOWNSTAIRS BRAIN OR DISTRACT YOU BY TALKING?

WOULD YOU RATHER HELP SOMEONE IN THEIR DOWNSTAIRS BRAIN OR FIND SOMEONE ELSE TO HELP?

WOULD YOU RATHER CRITICIZE SOMEONE WHEN THEY ARE HAVING BIG EMOTIONS OR SIT WITH THEM WHILE THEY GET BACK IN THEIR UPSTAIRS BRAIN?

WOULD YOU RATHER WAIT UNTIL SOMEONE IS BACK IN THEIR UPSTAIRS BRAIN TO HANG OUT WITH THEM OR DISCOVER WHY THEY ARE DYSREGULATING?

WOULD YOU RATHER QUIETLY LISTEN WHILE SOMEONE SHARES THEIR WORRIES OR SHARE IDEAS OF HOW THEY CAN FIX THE SITUATION?

We need joy as we need air. We need love as we need water. We need each other as we need the earth we share."

MAYA ANGELOU

CHAPTER 5

Braving Big Emotions

MIND MAP

On the board, draw a mind map and ask students to consider the meaning of *angry*.

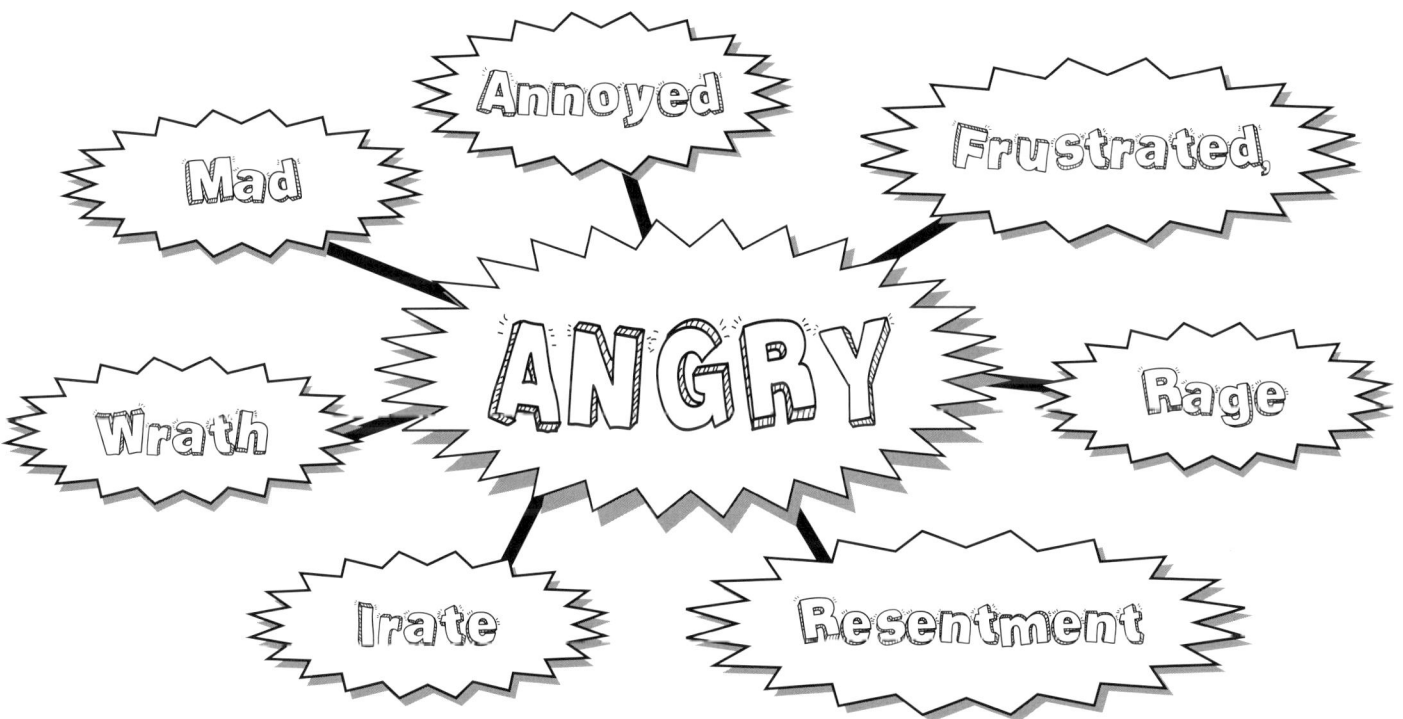

Annoyed

Mad

Frustrated,

Wrath

ANGRY

Rage

Irate

Resentment

ASCA® STANDARDS

- **B-LS 2.** Creative approach to learning tasks and problem-solving
- **B-SMS 2.** Self-discipline and self-control
- **B-SMS 7.** Effective coping skills
- **B-SS 9.** Social Maturity and behaviors appropriate to the situation and environment

In a small group format, complete a brief check-in with students by asking them to indicate their feelings using the brain stoplight check-in.

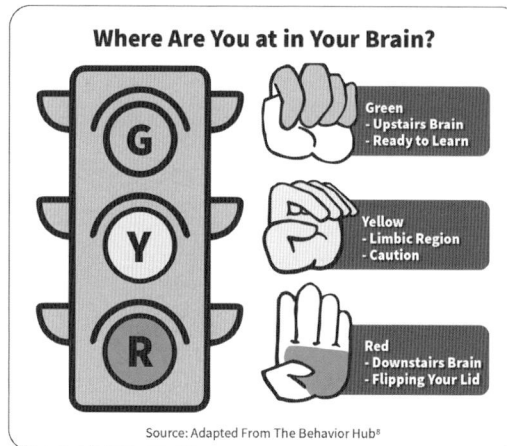

Where Are You at in Your Brain?

Green
- Upstairs Brain
- Ready to Learn

Yellow
- Limbic Region
- Caution

Red
- Downstairs Brain
- Flipping Your Lid

Source: Adapted From The Behavior Hub[8]

Review the Group Expectations before asking students to share their knowledge of the topic from the previous week. Ask students to share one thing they did differently this week because of what they learned in last week's lesson. (If you used the Additional Activities to give suggestions for when they feel disconnected, sad, or confused ask them if they tried the suggestions and how they worked.) Together, review the Mind Map. Then, read the Lesson Introduction and ask the Circle Time Questions before reading the Story and asking the Discussion Questions. Students can work in pairs to craft their responses or share with the whole group. Complete the Skill Practice, "Would You Rather?" Game and Additional Activities as time allows. Be sure to complete the Closing Considerations with each lesson.

LESSON INTRODUCTION

A person can feel many different emotions, ranging from mild to heavy. Some of the bigger emotions can get "mixed up and bubble over, exploding onto others.[1] When that happens, anger is usually at the root. Anger protects us from uncomfortable feelings by making us feel strong and in control."

When we feel angry, we naturally want to yell or hurt others, but those actions don't resolve things. They make things worse. We need to figure out what is hiding underneath the anger.

Consider the following emotions that might be the cause of anger:

- Embarrassment
- Loneliness
- Shame
- Fear

Ask students to reflect and share their answers to the following questions with the group. Larger groups may need to be broken into smaller groups to give students ample time to share their answers and deepen the conversation.

- What does it feel like, and what do you notice happening inside you when big emotions arise?
- What or who helps when you feel anger taking over?
- What do you think is mainly behind the anger when you get mad?

STORY TIME

Hand out coloring sheets and crayons or markers to younger students while the facilitator reads the story, if desired.

Name It to Tame It!

Ms. London asked Rachel and Robby to come to her office to talk about what had happened. They had gotten into a fight, and Ms. London wanted to get to the bottom of it.

"I don't want to talk about it," Rachel said, her arms crossed over her chest.

"I can understand that. Would it be all right if Robby shared his side first to give you some time?" Ms. London suggested.

"I guess," she replied sullenly, digging her heels into the floor.

"It's not my fault!" Robby piped up, "Rachel started it." Rachel let out a growl.

"Jamie told me that Rachel took my baseball glove. What was I supposed to do? I needed it for the game. My parents would have been so mad if I didn't bring it home. So, I told Rachel she better give it back or I was gonna take something of hers. She never gave it back, so I took her backpack. Then she started kicking me, so I pushed her away."

Ms. London asked Rachel if she was ready to share her side.

Reluctantly, Rachel started speaking quietly. "It was supposed to be a joke. Jamie told me it would be funny to hide Robby's mitt. I was gonna give it back, but when I went to get it, it was gone from where I had hidden it." There was a long pause. "I'm sorry, Robby. I kicked you because I was embarrassed and scared. I didn't know what to do when you took my backpack. I just reacted, and things got out of hand."

"Well, I have some good news." Ms. London told them, "Someone put the mitt in the lost and found." She handed it to Robby, who looked extremely relieved.

"I want to teach you a strategy that will help you when something happens and anger and other big emotions bubble over. Robby, you mentioned you were worried about your parents getting upset, and Rachel mentioned fear and embarrassment." She continued, "I want you both to think about how you felt walking here and how you feel now. I suspect that both of you feel better. Maybe you don't feel utterly joyful, but I doubt you are as worried." They both nodded in agreement.

"That's because you expressed your emotions and shared how you felt. You both took responsibility and were honest. When you name your feelings, that helps calm you, shifting you from your downstairs brain to your upstairs brain. We call that "Name it to Tame it."[2] Simply put, saying things out loud makes us feel better. Big emotions will happen again, and, hopefully, you both have learned from this. And now you have a new tool to help."

DISCUSSION QUESTIONS

- What feelings does the story highlight? What else might Robby and Rachel have felt?

- How did Rachel and Robby shift from downstairs to upstairs?

- What would you have done if someone took something valuable from you?

- Who could Rachel and Robby teach their new skill to?

SKILL PRACTICE

Direct the students to become Emotional Explorers. Encourage them to take turns reading the scenarios and accompanying questions to each other.

- Midway through a math test, Alex ran out of the room, slamming the door.

  - What else might be going on?

  - Is it possible that Alex was ashamed because he hadn't studied and knew he wouldn't get a good grade?

  - What could Alex have done instead?

- Bailey yelled at her mom when asked to finish her chores.

  - What else might be going on?

  - Could Bailey feel stressed because she had extra homework and worry she wouldn't have time to play after homework and chores?

  - What could Bailey have done instead?

- Julio shoved his brother out of the way right after they got home from baseball practice.

  - What else might be going on?

  - Is it possible that Julio felt embarrassed and rejected that his brother made the baseball team, and he didn't?

  - What could Julio have done instead?

- Mr. Elwood raised his voice at the class and gave them extra homework.

   - What else might be going on?

   - Could Mr. Elwood feel frustrated because his students weren't listening to him?

   - What could Mr. Elwood have done instead?

ADDITIONAL ACTIVITIES

- Let students know that sometimes big feelings get so overwhelming they don't feel survivable. But emotions are like clouds that float in the sky. They change their shape and float away. They aren't permanent. Emotions will pass. Assure students that feelings and emotions change. The ways they feel during big moments of dysregulation won't last forever. Validate their emotions, encourage them to draw their feelings, express what they feel or have felt, and then imagine that they are on their back looking up at the sky, watching the emotions drift away.

- Play a game in which students take turns acting out a combination of two animals that are very different from each other. Everyone takes a turn guessing the two animals. Make up a funny name combo if students need a hint. For example, shamel=shark and camel, or parkey=parrot and monkey, or hant=horse and ant. (Explain that laughter and movement are two of the best ways to relieve stress.)

CLOSING CONSIDERATIONS

Let students know that everyone has hard days, flips their lid, and experiences big emotions. You don't have to deal with big feelings alone, and you don't have to get stuck in them. Labeling and expressing the feeling will help, along with other strategies you have learned and will learn in upcoming sessions, like anchoring, asking for help, and using buffers.

Ask students to summarize the content of this session's lesson in one sentence.

Ask students to consider a recent time when they felt a big emotion and what could have been underneath that feeling. What was the emotion communicating? Encourage them to be intentional about noticing their feelings this week and to try labeling and naming those feelings as they arise. In pairs or groups of three, students may share their answers. If time allows, a few students may share with the whole group.

Playing the "Would You Rather?" game is a fun and engaging activity for students to develop their critical thinking skills. Students will reflect on their experience, evaluate their options based on their preferences, and reflect on the opinions of others, providing a different perspective and strengthening their sense of connection to one another.

Would You Rather?

Copy and cut out the questions for small groups to discuss, or have each person stand in the center of the room and move towards one side or the other to show their vote for either option as the facilitator reads the questions aloud.

WOULD YOU RATHER IGNORE YOUR FEELINGS, HOPING THEY PASS, OR DEAL WITH THEM BY TALKING ABOUT THEM?

WOULD YOU RATHER NAME YOUR FEELINGS OUT LOUD OR WRITE THEM OUT?

WOULD YOU RATHER FIGURE OUT WHAT IS UNDERNEATH THE EMOTION ON YOUR OWN OR HAVE SOMEONE HELP YOU DO SO?

WOULD YOU RATHER APOLOGIZE FIRST OR APOLOGIZE AFTER SOMEONE ELSE GOES FIRST?

WOULD YOU RATHER HELP SOMEONE FIGURE OUT HOW TO MANAGE THEIR BIG EMOTIONS OR BE AN EXAMPLE AND MODEL HOW TO HANDLE THEM?

WOULD YOU RATHER CRY ALONE OR WITH SOMEONE WHEN YOU FEEL SAD?

NAME IT TO TAME IT

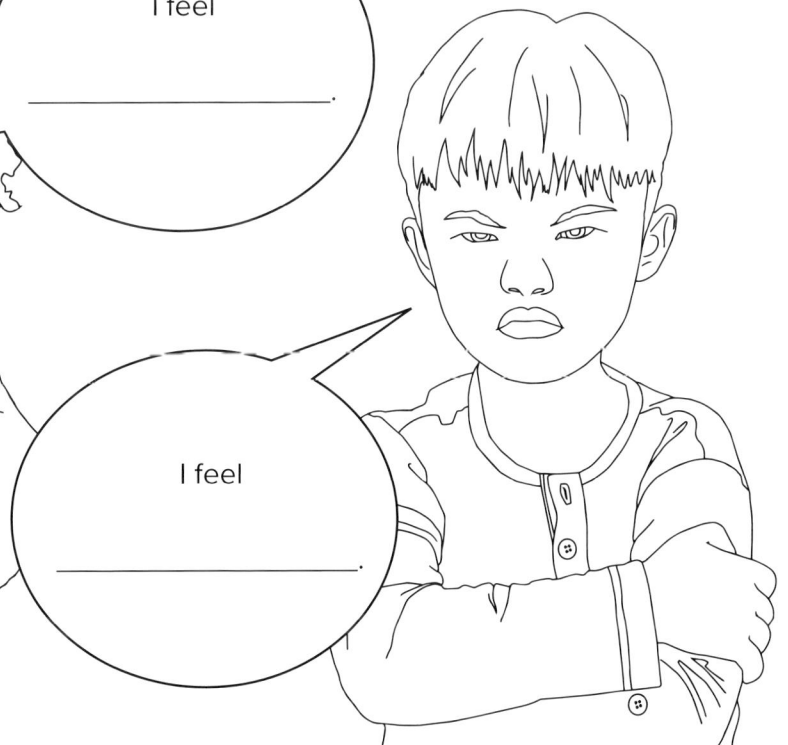

I feel

_____.

I feel

_____.

I feel

_____.

I feel

_____.

CHAPTER 6

Stress Busting

MIND MAP

On the board, draw a mind map and ask students to consider the meaning of *stress*.

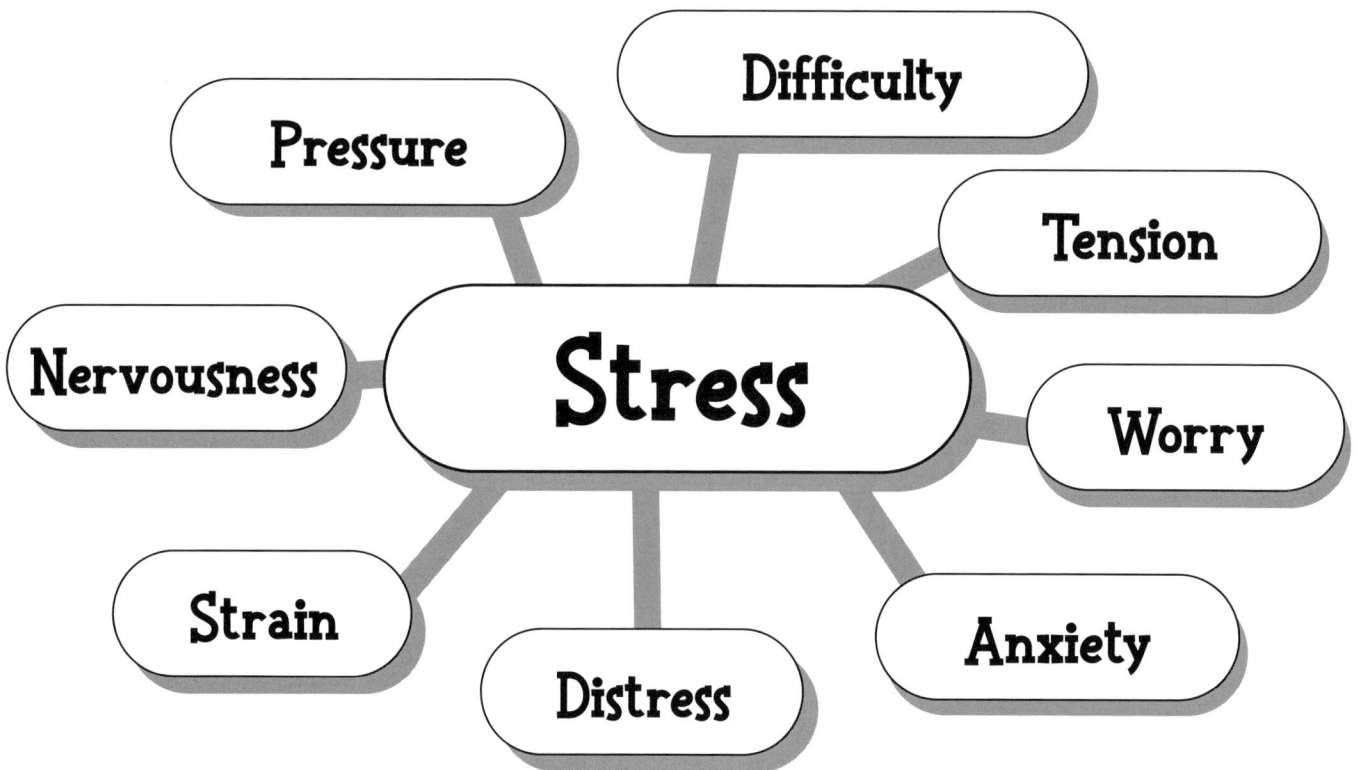

ASCA® STANDARDS

- **B-LS 3.** Time management, organizational, and study skills
- **B-SMS 6.** Ability to identify and overcome barriers
- **B-SMS 8.** Balance of school, home, and community activities
- **B-SS 8.** Advocacy Skills for self and others and ability to assert self, when necessary

In a small group format, complete a brief check-in with students by asking them to indicate their feelings using the brain stoplight check-in.

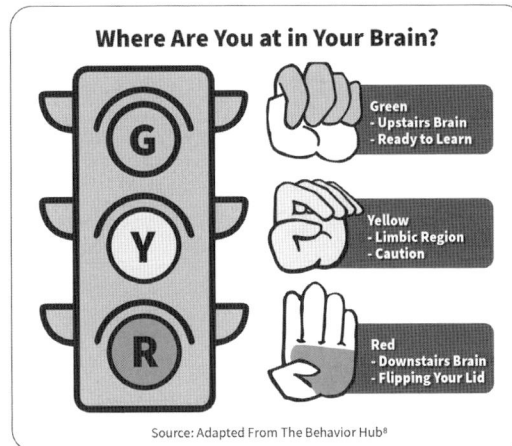

Where Are You at in Your Brain?

G
Green
- Upstairs Brain
- Ready to Learn

Y
Yellow
- Limbic Region
- Caution

R
Red
- Downstairs Brain
- Flipping Your Lid

Source: Adapted From The Behavior Hub®

Review the Group Expectations before asking students to share their knowledge of the topic from the previous week. Ask students to share one thing they did differently this week because of what they learned in last week's lesson. Together, review the Mind Map. Then, read the Lesson Introduction and ask the Circle Time Questions before reading the Story and the Discussion Questions. Students can work in pairs to craft their responses or share with the whole group. Complete the Skill Practice, "Would You Rather?" game, and Additional Activities as time allows. Be sure to complete the Closing Considerations with each lesson.

LESSON INTRODUCTION

Introduce the subject for the week by defining stress.

Stress is the shift that happens in your body when you encounter something that makes you feel overwhelmed or unsafe. Not all stress is bad and not all stress lasts. We need a little stress each day to help us get out of bed and accomplish what we need to do. But if the stress doesn't go away, it can become toxic and be very harmful to our physical and emotional health. We don't need to be afraid of stress. There are things we can do to reduce it and shield ourselves from harmful effects. We can avoid getting stuck when we fear failure, struggle with perfectionism, or are overwhelmed with school or other demands.

Stress relieving suggestions:

- Movement/Exercise/Play

- Deep Breathing

- Spending time with friends and family

- Laughter

- Love and Affection

- Crying

- Being creative

Ask students to reflect and share their answers to the following questions with the group. Larger groups may need to be broken into smaller groups to give students ample time to share their answers and deepen the conversation.

- What stresses you out?

- What or who helps ease your stress and worries?

- What do you do when you feel stuck?

STORY TIME

Hand out coloring sheets and crayons or markers to younger students while the facilitator reads the story, if desired.

Stressed Out!

Izzy couldn't wait to get on the bus and go home. She had felt distracted all day. She had difficulty concentrating on her school lessons because she kept thinking about what her dad told her last night. He let the family know that his company was downsizing, and he needed to find a new job. Dad kept saying, "Don't worry!" but the more he said that the more worried Izzy became. Her heart started racing again, "What if we have to move? What if we can't still go on vacation? What if ...?" So many what-ifs were swirling in her head! The more Izzy thought about it, the bigger her stress felt.

The bus was starting to fill up with kids. The noise level got louder and louder, and the sticky, hot air felt suffocating. Izzy thought she might pass out. Sofia noticed Izzy was fidgeting and trying to fan herself. Sofia moved over to Izzy's bus seat and put the window down to let more air in. Sofia whispered, "Izzy, are you okay?"

Izzy's eyes welled up with tears, and Sofia hugged her friend and said, "You don't have to talk about it if you don't want to." They sat silently for a few minutes, and then Izzy shared her worries with Sofia.

Sofia listened. She wasn't sure what to say, but she remembered times when she felt overwhelmed, and it was hard to describe her feelings. Her mom listened and just sat with her. The most interesting thing about that experience was that even though her mom couldn't fix her problem, Sofia still felt better. Something about her mom being with her was enough to help her not feel as scared because she was not alone. She hoped she could do that for Izzy, too.

When they got to Izzy's bus stop, Izzy sighed and said, "I feel a little better. Thanks for sitting with me." She gave Sofia a fist bump and walked up her driveway, where her puppy, Rocky, was waiting for her.

He jumped into her arms, almost knocking her over! She laughed as he licked her face. How did he know she needed his fuzzy cuddles? Izzy let out another big sigh. She was still slightly worried but felt stronger and knew she could talk to her friend and family and snuggle Rocky if the overwhelming feelings started again.

DISCUSSION QUESTIONS

- How did Sofia know that Izzy needed help, and what did she do to help?

- What do you think helped Izzy start to feel better?

- What might have happened if Sofia hadn't offered help?

- What could both Izzy and Sofia have done that could make things worse?

SKILL PRACTICE

Let's learn about buffers. A buffer is a person, activity, or object that lessens the impact of stress or danger by preventing direct contact with something or someone harmful. Buffers cushion the blow (imagine how bubble wrap protects a fragile item). Buffers are tools that help us manage stress and shield us from adversity by soothing and calming us. Buffers have our backs, speak up for us, and teach us how to manage our problems, making us feel safe. They lift our worries, make us laugh, and challenge us to grow and do hard things. Buffers make us feel better both immediately and in a long-term healthy way. Let's talk about different kinds of buffers.

Signal by raising your hand if any of these buffers help you handle stress:

- A relative

- A friend

- A coach

- A teacher

- A neighbor

- Your pet

- Eating healthy and getting enough sleep

- Playing outside

- Playing sports

- Playing or listening to music

- Deep breathing

- Journaling

- Making something/crafting

- Drawing or painting

- Watching a funny show

- Talking to someone, sharing your feelings

- A weighted blanket or hug/something heavy that gives pressure

- Direct students to stand up for each item or situation that can increase stress. Encourage them to share a positive replacement.

  - Energy drinks and too much candy

  - Staying inside all day

  - Staying up past bedtime

  - Using drugs

  - Eating unhealthy food or skipping meals

  - Telling people what they want to hear instead of the truth

  - Listening to people complain

  - Spending too much time online

- Direct students to visualize a rocket taking off to the moon. Tell them to take a deep breath as you count them down (3.2.1.) to lift off. On the exhale direct them to let out a loud explosion of air as the rocket launches into space. Repeat making the exhale long and slow.

CLOSING CONSIDERATIONS

Life will never be perfectly calm and peaceful. We will encounter stressful bumps in the road, which is ok because we are not meant to be heartless robots. Stress is not the problem. We can manage our stress. We can put coping strategies and buffers into place that will help us rather than make things worse! Some things are out of our control, but buffers can also help us.

Ask students to summarize the content of this session's lesson in one sentence.

Ask students to consider things that help them feel better and worse, and to be intentional about noticing the choices that help or hurt them this week. Encourage them to consider what buffers their stress and find that person and activity that will help them throughout the week when they encounter stressful moments. In pairs or groups of three, students may share their answers. If time allows, a few students may share with the whole group.

Playing the "Would You Rather?" game is a fun and engaging activity for students to develop their critical thinking skills. Students will reflect on their experience, evaluate their options based on their preferences, and reflect on the opinions of others, providing a different perspective and strengthening their sense of connection to one another.

Would You Rather?

Copy and cut out the questions for small groups to discuss, or have each person stand in the center of the room and move towards one side or the other to show their vote for either option as the facilitator reads the questions aloud.

WHEN YOU FEEL STRESSED, WOULD YOU RATHER SUFFER IN SILENCE OR ASK FOR HELP?

WHEN YOU FEEL STRESSED, WOULD YOU RATHER SPEND TIME WITH A PET OR TALK TO AN ADULT?

WOULD YOU RATHER SHARE WITH A FRIEND WHAT HELPS YOU HANDLE STRESS OR LET THAT FRIEND FIGURE IT OUT ON THEIR OWN?

WOULD YOU RATHER PLAY A SPORT WITH A TEAM OR DO THINGS BY YOURSELF?

WOULD YOU RATHER SEE IF THE STRESS WILL DISAPPEAR WITH TIME OR IMMEDIATELY ASK FOR HELP?

WOULD YOU RATHER BE SOMEONE'S "BUFFER" WHEN THEY ARE STRESSED OUT OR HAVE SOMEONE ELSE HELP THEM?

Circle any picture(s) that represent ways to protect and buffer your stress. If you have other ideas, draw them on a separate sheet of paper.

ANCHORS

MIND MAP

On the board, draw a mind map and ask students to consider the meaning of *anchor*.

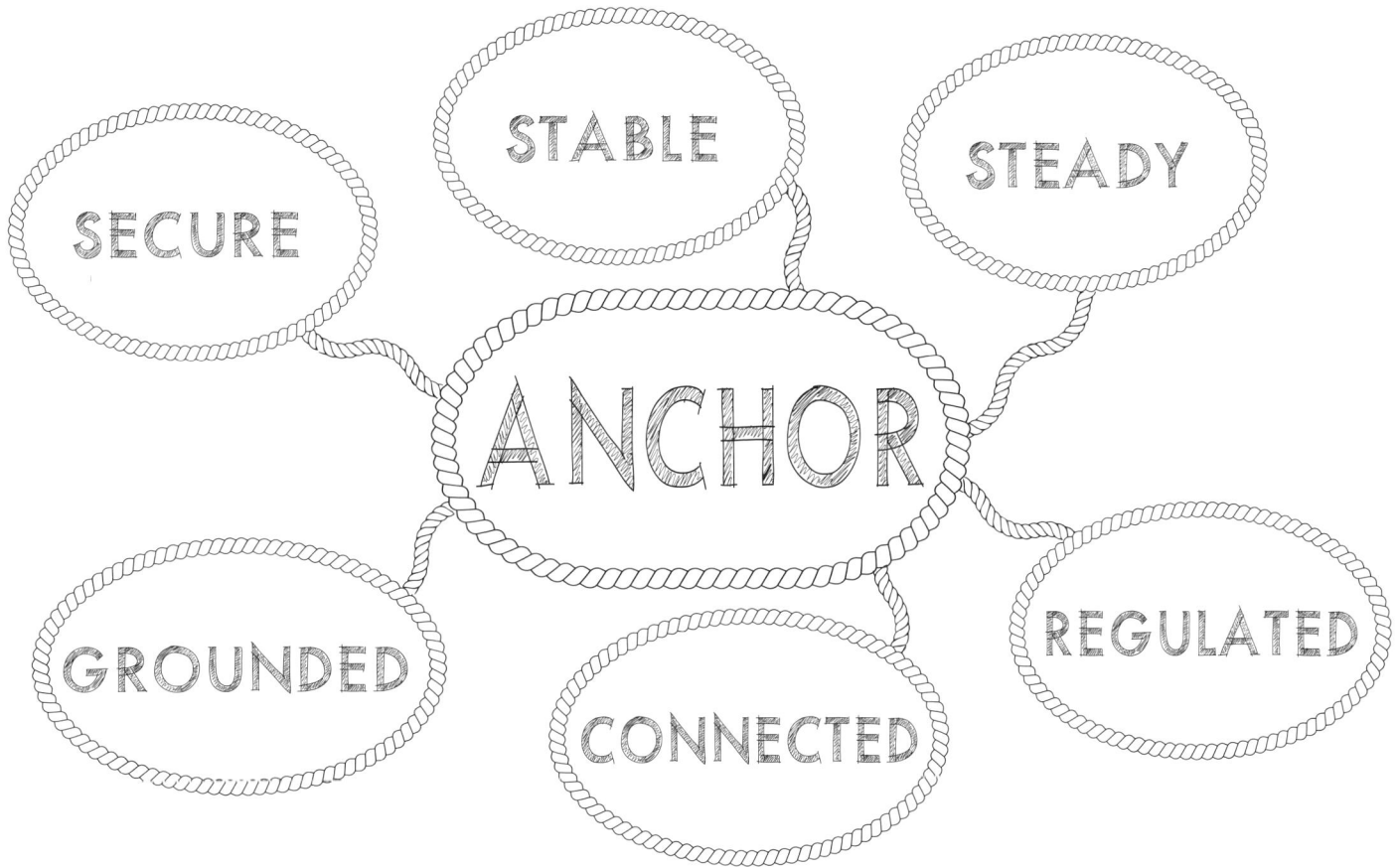

SECURE

STABLE

STEADY

ANCHOR

GROUNDED

CONNECTED

REGULATED

ASCA® STANDARDS

- **B-LS 2.** Creative approach to learning, tasks, and problem-solving
- **B-SMS 7.** Effective coping skills
- **B-SMS 10.** Ability to manage transitions and adapt to change
- **B-SS 9.** Social maturity and behaviors appropriate to the situation and environment

In a small group format, complete a brief check-in with students by asking them to indicate their feelings using the brain stoplight check-in.

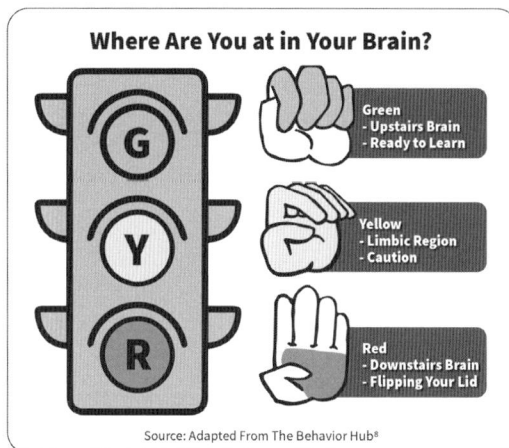

Where Are You at in Your Brain?

Green
- Upstairs Brain
- Ready to Learn

Yellow
- Limbic Region
- Caution

Red
- Downstairs Brain
- Flipping Your Lid

Source: Adapted From The Behavior Hub®

Review the Group Expectations before asking students to share their knowledge of the topic from the previous week. Ask students to share one thing they did differently this week because of what they learned in last week's lesson. Together, review the Mind Map. Then, read the Lesson Introduction and ask the Circle Time Questions before reading the Story and asking the Discussion Questions. Students can work in pairs to craft their responses or share with the whole group. Complete the Skill Practice, "Would You Rather?" game, and Additional Activities as time allows. Be sure to complete the Closing Considerations with each lesson.

LESSON INTRODUCTION

Introduce the subject for the week by defining anchoring.

Anchoring: An anchor holds an object firmly, like a boat anchored to the ocean floor, so it won't drift away or be tossed around in a storm. An anchor is supportive and reliable and holds you steady. Anchoring strategies help you manage big emotions and move from your downstairs brain to your upstairs brain. As you learned in the previous lesson, stress is "the shift that happens in your body when you encounter something that makes you feel overwhelmed or unsafe." Anchors help your body and brain feel safe again. An anchor can be a person, thing, a belief, place, or memory that helps you feel more grounded and stable.

Examples of anchoring are spending time with a favorite person, holding a special object, and thinking of a warm memory or beloved person. All of these examples help create a sense of security and stability—the opposite of the insecurity and instability caused by stress!

CIRCLE TIME QUESTIONS

Ask students to reflect and share their answers to the following questions with the group. Larger groups may need to be broken into smaller groups to give students ample time to share their answers and deepen the conversation.

- Have you ever felt overwhelmed, as if you were being tossed around in an ocean and were drowning? What was that like?

- Have you ever felt steady and balanced with your emotions like you were anchored? What was that like?

- Have you ever thought that a person, pet, hobby, or memory could help you feel safe and in control when you are overwhelmed in your downstairs brain? Give an example.

STORY TIME

Hand out coloring sheets and crayons or markers to younger students while the facilitator reads the story, if desired.

Amazing Anchoring Otters

Diego woke up early Saturday morning, ready to go hiking with his buddy, Dallin. They had been planning this hike for what seemed like forever, and finally, the day had come. Diego wolfed down his breakfast and ran across the street to see if Dallin was ready to go. Dallin was eagerly waiting on his doorstep, anxious to get the hike started. The boys helped Diego's dad load their backpacks, and they were off. When they finally arrived at the trailhead, they unloaded their gear and started on the path. Diego's dad told them not to go too far ahead and stay together. He would follow behind. They winked at each other, hoping to reach the peak long before Diego's father could.

Even though the weatherman said it would be a sunny day, clouds began to appear. Then came the rain. At first, it seemed like a muddy adventure, but soon, it was pouring, and the trail began to wash away. It wasn't long before the boys realized they couldn't see any path ahead. They were lost.

"Are you scared?" Diego asked. "A little," Dallin sheepishly replied as his foot sunk into a mudhole. Diego called out for his dad, but there was no response. The boys sat down next to a fallen tree for protection from the wind and rain. They were out of breath from staying upright and steady on the slippery mountain slope.

Dallin perked up, "I just thought of something that might help us!" Diego leaned in to listen as lightning crackled overhead. "Gemma and I learned about otters last week." Diego rolled his eyes, "I don't think otters are gonna save us up here!"

Dallin continued, "Otters do this cool thing during storms called anchoring. They stick themselves to the ocean floor, so they don't get tossed around in storms. Mother otters wrap their babies in kelp so the pup will stay in one place while she is diving for food. Otters also hold tight to each other, so they don't drift away."

Diego looked confused, "I don't have any kelp!"

Dallin's dad was the safest person he could think of, and just remembering what his dad had taught him made Dallin feel a little better. "My dad told me if we get caught out in a storm, the biggest danger is lightning, so we should find a low spot that's not near any tall trees or standing water and hunker down with our ponchos until dad catches up with us."

They found a low spot just beside the trail, away from tall trees and standing water, opened their backpacks, and pulled out their ponchos. Dallin turned to Diego, "Dad also said to sit so you're a ball, with your feet touching one another. Being huddled up together will help us stay warm." They both got into position and then waited and continued to call out for Diego's dad. Dallin pulled out his favorite pocket stone that his dad gave him and rubbed it. He shared it with Diego. They both felt calmer, taking turns with the stone, talking about what both their dads had taught them about the outdoors, and imagining themselves as otters, anchored to the bottom of a stormy ocean. Just holding the stone, staying together, and talking made the storm seem less scary.

Suddenly, a voice could be faintly heard calling their names. Around the bend, Diego's father appeared, looking very worried and very wet.

"I am so glad you boys are ok!" He noticed how they'd taken shelter and relied on one another. "Brilliant!" he exclaimed. "You used your heads and leaned on each other for support."

"Otters for the win!" shouted Diego. His dad looked confused, and Diego laughed, "We'll tell you all about it on the drive home!"

DISCUSSION QUESTIONS

- How did the boys anchor themselves during the storm?
- What other strategies did they use to keep calm and safe?
- How do you know they were in their upstairs brain during the story?
- What storms in your life do you need an otter buddy and anchoring for?
- What else could the boys have done in that situation?

SKILL PRACTICE

Ask students to pretend to be news reporters and interview each other, asking the following questions.

- Who is supportive and makes you feel safe (could be a pet or someone who has passed away).
- What makes you feel cozy or alive and steadies you? (Helps move you from downstairs to upstairs brain).
- Where is someplace(s) that brings good memories, makes you feel safe, and helps you feel connected?
- What is a memory where you felt steady, capable, strong, and comforted?

ADDITIONAL ACTIVITIES

- Tell students that there are different ways to move from their downstairs to upstairs brains. Read the list aloud and encourage students to try at least one idea from the three sections below.
  - When you feel disconnected or dizzy:

- Press your back firmly against the wall or while lying down

    - Jump up and down

    - Tighten your muscles, hold, then release

  - When you feel sad or worried:

    - Think about a favorite memory with your pet or best friend

    - Hum a favorite song

    - Think about something you are looking forward to

  - When you feel confused and can't think clearly:

    - Count by 5s to 100

    - Think of a friend and spell their name out loud

    - Think of an animal for every letter of the alphabet

- Lead the students in the following visualization:

"Lake Float"

Close your eyes if you feel comfortable.

Imagine a cloudy sky. Notice the clouds floating away, revealing the sun's rays lighting everything you see.

You notice a lake next to you and grab an inner tube so you can float.

You dip a toe into the lake and step down, feeling the cool water touch your warm skin. The sunshine makes you feel so good inside. You jump up on your tube and begin to float.

You glide your fingers in the water, making circles and swirls.

You smile because you feel so calm and grateful for this relaxing moment.

What is around you to notice? Are there trees, animals, or people you love?

You might find yourself especially thankful for this day, knowing there will never be another day like today. Each day is different; you feel happy because life is an adventure.

You now notice that your float is over, and it is time to leave the water.

Now, it's time to gather your thoughts and remember how you felt when you returned to your room.

When you're ready, open your eyes and take a deep breath, followed by a long, slow exhale!

CLOSING CONSIDERATIONS

Anchors can help us when we are in our downstairs brain and have big emotions. We can think of a happy memory, talk to someone who anchors us, or do a grounding meditation like the one above, helping us feel steady and firm. Ask students to summarize the content of this session's lesson in one sentence.

Ask students to consider what tools and strategies they can try this week that they haven't tried yet. Encourage them to consider their anchors. Students may share their answers in pairs or groups of three. If time allows, a few students may share with the whole group.

Playing the "Would You Rather?" game is a fun and engaging activity for students to develop their critical thinking skills. Students will reflect on their experience, evaluate their options based on their preferences, and reflect on the opinions of others, providing a different perspective and strengthening their sense of connection to one another.

WOULD YOU RATHER?

Copy and cut out the questions for small groups to discuss, or have each person stand in the center of the room and move towards one side or the other to show their vote for either option as the facilitator reads the questions aloud.

WOULD YOU RATHER TRY AN ANCHORING TECHNIQUE OR A DIFFERENT EMOTIONAL MANAGEMENT STRATEGY?

WOULD YOU RATHER RELY ON A PERSON OR MEMORY TO ANCHOR YOU?

WOULD YOU RATHER WALK BAREFOOT OUTSIDE OR HOLD AN ICE CUBE TO FEEL BETTER?

WOULD YOU RATHER GET TOSSED AROUND IN A STORM, ON A BOAT, WITHOUT AN ANCHOR OR WALK ON SHIFTING, UNSTEADY GROUND?

WOULD YOU RATHER HANDLE YOUR LIFE'S STORMS ALONE OR WITH STRATEGIES LIKE ANCHORS?

WOULD YOU RATHER BE SOMEONE'S ANCHOR WHEN THEY ARE STRUGGLING OR HAVE SOMEONE ELSE HELP THEM?

Something that makes me feel safe and secure is _____

I feel safe and secure in _____

I feel safe and secure when _____

I feel safe and secure with _____

First Aid for Feelings

MIND MAP

On the board, draw a mind map and ask students to consider the meaning of *prevention*.

anticipate

get ahead of

avoid

Prevention

pro-active

deter

watch out for

ASCA® STANDARDS

- **B-LS 2.** Creative approach to learning, tasks, and problem-solving
- **B-SMS 6.** Ability to identify and overcome barriers
- **B-SMS 10.** Ability to manage transitions and adapt to change
- **B-SS 3.** Positive relationships with adults to support success

In a small group format, complete a brief check-in with students by asking them to indicate their feelings using the brain stoplight check-in.

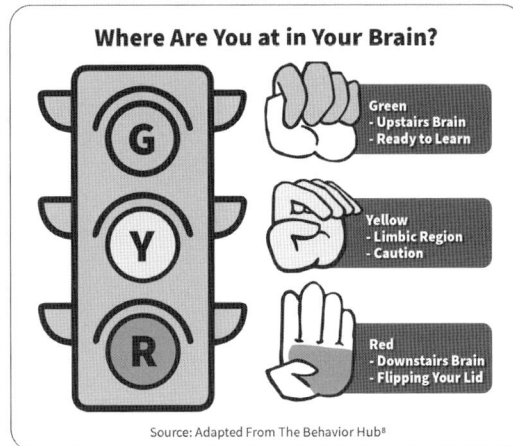

Where Are You at in Your Brain?

Green
- Upstairs Brain
- Ready to Learn

Yellow
- Limbic Region
- Caution

Red
- Downstairs Brain
- Flipping Your Lid

Source: Adapted From The Behavior Hub®

Review the Group Expectations before asking students to share their knowledge of the topic from the previous week. Ask students to share one thing they did differently during the past week because of what they learned in last week's lesson. Together, review the Mind Map. Then, read the Lesson Introduction and ask the Circle Time Questions before reading the Story and the Discussion Questions. Students can work in pairs to craft their responses or share with the whole group. Complete the Skill Practice, "Would You Rather?" game, and Additional Activities as time allows. Be sure to complete the Closing Considerations with each lesson.

LESSON INTRODUCTION

Introduce the subject for the week by reminding students about preventing emotional outbursts and shutdowns. Managing emotions requires skills that take a long time to build. Students need help and years of positive, safe moments with others before they should be expected to manage emotions without help. Prevention will help get them to the point where they can be self-advocates and recognize what they need to navigate feelings and sensations. Creating an emotional rescue plan is the first step in becoming able to handle and modulate difficult emotional situations on their own.

A Feelings First Aid Plan helps us identify triggers—things that activate our nervous system, causing us to flip our lid. A rescue plan helps implement tools and strategies that help us feel better in our downstairs brain. The plan could include:

- A safe place to go
- A safe person to talk to
- Favorite breathing techniques
- Favorite affirmations

Challenge students to think about what else could go there.

Ask students to reflect and share their answers to the following questions with the group. Larger groups may need to be broken into smaller groups to give students ample time to share their answers and deepen the conversation.

- What irritates, bothers, and frustrates you, sending you to your downstairs brain?

- What do you notice when you feel irritated, bothered, or frustrated?

- What helps you when you feel sad, angry, overwhelmed, or frustrated?

STORY TIME

Hand out coloring sheets and crayons or markers to younger students while the facilitator reads the story, if desired.

Feelings First Aid to the Rescue

Nurse Brady taught the students how to manage their physical health during Health class. He showed them a first aid kit and how to use it. As he wrapped up his lesson, he said, "If you take care of your health, you won't get sick as often. You need to know what places and things are unsafe and can hurt. Oh, and one more thing: It's crucial to eat healthy, get sleep, exercise a little each day, and have a safety buddy with you."

After Nurse Brady left, Ms. Denning told the class that what he taught was true not only for their physical health but also for their emotional health. The confused look on the students' faces told her she needed to explain further.

"Let's imagine a first aid kit that could help you move from your downstairs brain to your upstairs brain. What would be in it?" she questioned the class.

Cassie timidly raised her hand. "What about lion breathing, where you roar on the exhale? That always makes me feel stronger when I am struggling. Is that what you mean?"

"That is a great answer. Breathing is an excellent item to include in our regulation first aid kit! What other tools could be in your first aid kits, class?" she asked.

Sebastian waved at Ms. Denning and said, "I always feel better after we have movement breaks!"

Ms. Denning smiled wide and responded. "Yes, Sebastian, I have noticed you all seem to do better after getting your wiggles out. I think you guys are getting it! The upstairs brain first aid kit would be full of tools and strategies like anchoring, movement, noticing what your body is telling you, and asking for help when needed. That's how we shift from downstairs to upstairs; the more we do that, the easier it becomes to prevent dysregulation. Knowing what bothers and irritates you can help you know that you need to do something to feel better. I also like what Nurse Brady said about avoiding places and things that are unsafe and can hurt you. How can we compare that to our emotional health?"

Jake raised his hand and said, "Well, some people are safe to be around so they can be our otter buddies!"

"Excellent, Jake," Ms. Denning approached him, "What else?" Jake continued, "Nurse Brady also said that we should eat healthy and get sleep, and I think it's good advice because I get more done when I am not tired."

Travis cut in, "Yeah, and remember when we learned that sugar and caffeine make anxiety worse?"

"Oh, I love that you have been listening and learning in class!" Ms. Denning addressed them all. You have been creating your Feelings First Aid kit for prevention and intervention this whole year. Keep adding to it, find what works, and you will be able to help yourself when you need it!"

DISCUSSION QUESTIONS

- What advice did Ms. Denning give to the class, and how can you incorporate it into your life?
- In what ways do our physical health and emotional health overlap?
- What tools that the students mentioned could be in their first aid kits?
- What else could you add to your Feelings First Aid kit

SKILL PRACTICE

Emotional Antibiotics

Teach the students that emotional injuries can become infected if not treated just as we would treat any other infection. Antibiotics help heal infections. When your heart breaks, you may feel intense butterflies or choked up. How can we take an emotional antibiotic to prevent it from worsening and help it heal?

Direct students to listen to the following and give a thumbs-up if the item would be an emotional antibiotic and a thumbs-down if it could make the wound infected (mix them up).

Thumbs-Up list / Ointment and Bandage:

- A pet
- Journaling/drawing
- Water and a snack
- Talking to a friend
- Getting more sleep
- Eating healthy
- Exercise
- Taking a brain break

Thumbs-Down list / Infection:

- Ignoring your feelings

- Staying up late

- Eating junk food

- Playing video games for hours

- Gossiping about a classmate

- Lying to avoid getting in trouble

- Yelling at your sister when she takes your stuff

- Skipping breakfast

ADDITIONAL ACTIVITIES

- Let the students know that movement is the quickest and most efficient way to prevent big emotions from taking over! Turn on some fun music and take turns teaching each other your favorite dance moves. You make it more fun and incorporate laughter and silliness—which also dispels stress hormones—by playing slow music for fast dance moves and fast music for slow moves. Tell them to notice how they feel before and after.

- Direct students to write their worries or fears on paper and then fold them into a paper boat. Discuss with them that they are going to imagine their paper boat floating down a river, away from them. Encourage them to visualize the worry losing power the further it floats away. They can take their paper boats home and float them, or you can keep them safe.

CLOSING CONSIDERATIONS

Teach students they don't have to heal their emotional injuries alone. They can always ask for help. When students know they are not alone and can collaborate with adults to develop tools and strategies, it will lead them to emotionally-healing choices and solutions. Remind them to be compassionate to themselves and foster strong emotional and physical health throughout their lives.

Ask students to consider what they already have in their emotional first aid kits that they can implement when they feel dysregulated and encourage them to add new strategies as well. Let them know that their emotional first aid kit may look different from others because what works for one person may not work for another, and that's ok. This is an exercise in learning to listen to what your brain and nervous system are telling you.

Playing the "Would You Rather?" game is a fun and engaging activity for students to develop their critical thinking skills. Students will reflect on their experience, evaluate their options based on their preferences, and reflect on the opinions of others, providing a different perspective and strengthening their sense of connection to one another.

Would You Rather?

Copy and cut out the questions for small groups to discuss, or have each person stand in the center of the room and move towards one side or the other to show their vote for either option as the facilitator reads the questions aloud.

WOULD YOU RATHER PREVENT EMOTIONAL INJURY OR RESPOND WITH YOUR FEELING FIRST AID KIT?

WOULD YOU RATHER BORROW FROM SOMEONE ELSE'S FEELING FIRST AID KIT OR USE YOUR OWN?

WOULD YOU RATHER WORK ON STRENGTHENING YOUR PHYSICAL HEALTH OR YOUR EMOTIONAL HEALTH?

WOULD YOU RATHER EAT HEALTHIER OR BINGE ON SNACKS?

WOULD YOU RATHER WATCH YOUR FAVORITE MOVIE LATE OR GO TO BED EARLY?

WOULD YOU RATHER HAVE ONE SOLID STRATEGY THAT WORKS BEST FOR YOU OR SEVERAL THAT WORK FAIRLY WELL?

I can soothe and heal my emotional injuries!

First Aid Kit

CHAPTER 9

MENDING MISTAKES

MIND MAP

On the board, draw a mind map and ask students to consider the meaning of *repair*.

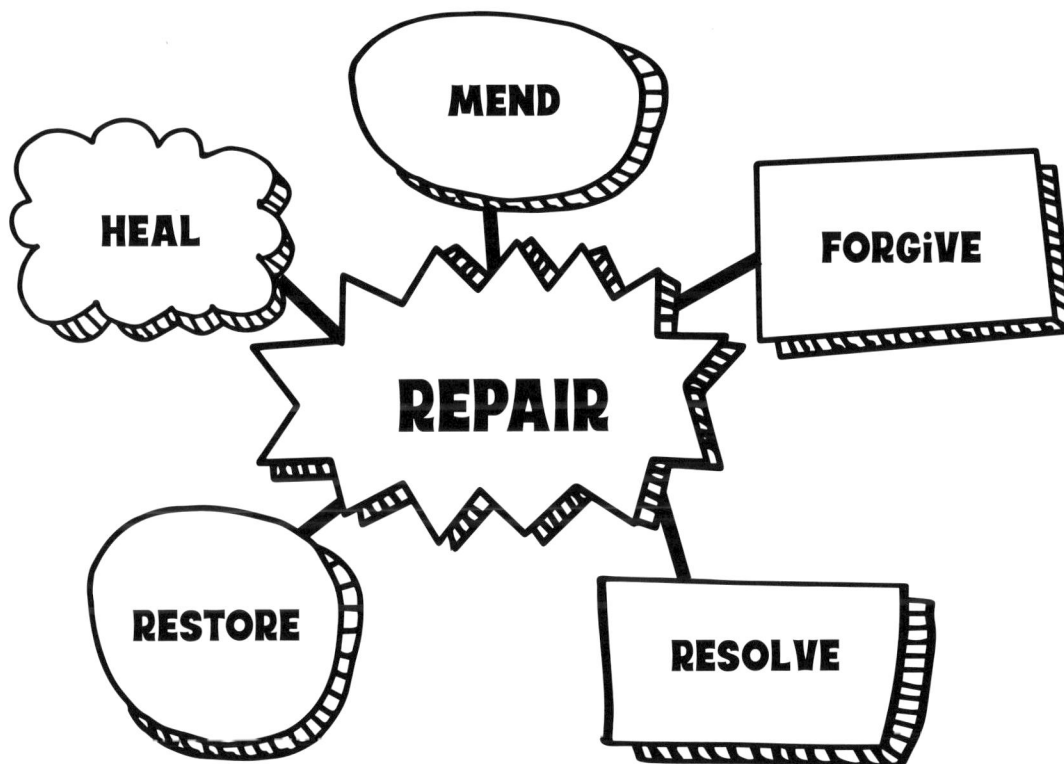

```
        MEND
HEAL          FORGIVE
      REPAIR
RESTORE        RESOLVE
```

ASCA® STANDARDS

- **B-LS 9.** Decision-making informed by gathering evidence, getting others' perspectives, and recognizing personal bias
- **B-SMS 1.** Responsibility for self and actions
- **B-SS 1.** Effective oral and written communication skills and listening skills
- **B-SS 5.** Ethical decision-making and social responsibility

In a small group format, complete a brief check-in with students by asking them to indicate their feelings using the brain stoplight check-in.

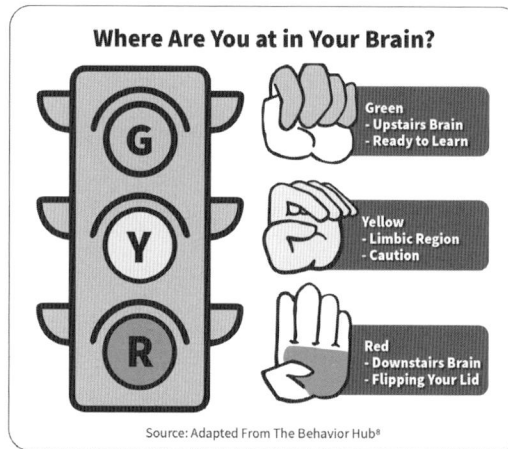

Where Are You at in Your Brain?

Green
- Upstairs Brain
- Ready to Learn

Yellow
- Limbic Region
- Caution

Red
- Downstairs Brain
- Flipping Your Lid

Source: Adapted From The Behavior Hub®

Review the Group Expectations before asking students to share their knowledge of the topic from the previous week. Ask students to share one thing they did differently this week because of what they learned in last week's lesson. Together, review the Mind Map. Then, read the Lesson Introduction and ask the Circle Time Questions before reading the Story and the Discussion Questions. Students can work in pairs to craft their responses or share with the whole group. Complete the Skill Practice, "Would You Rather?" game, and Additional Activities as time allows. Be sure to complete the Closing Considerations with each lesson.

LESSON INTRODUCTION

Everyone makes mistakes; it is a human thing. We aren't meant to be perfect. We can grow and learn when we mess up. We can repair harm and restore what was ruptured. It's about understanding the impact of our mistakes and resolving problems that arise from the errors we cause. We can be thoughtful in our decisions and forgive in order to build better, stronger relationships. What is broken can be fixed.

CIRCLE TIME QUESTIONS

Ask students to reflect and share their answers to the following questions with the group. Larger groups may need to be broken into smaller groups to give students ample time to share their answers and deepen the conversation.

- Why is apologizing such a complex and scary thing?

- Is it easier to forgive others or forgive yourself? Why?

- If an apology is forced or insincere, does it count? Why or why not?

Hand out coloring sheets and crayons or markers to younger students while the facilitator reads the story, if desired.

A Fraction of a Problem

On Thursday, Miss Stewart announced that there would be a test on fractions the following day. Quincy let out an audible groan. He hated fractions. No matter how hard he studied, he just didn't understand them.

When he got home, his dad could tell he was stressed. "I just know I will fail that test. Fractions are not my friend!" His dad patted his back, made him a grilled cheese sandwich, and tried comforting him. "Quincy, the most we can ask of you is to try your hardest. If you honestly do your best, that is enough."

The next day, Miss Stewart handed out the tests and let the students know that the printer had printed them out in lighter ink. When Quincy started the test, he wrote the wrong number and began erasing it. He quickly realized that the whole problem was being erased along with his pencil marks.

An idea instantly came to him. He could erase and modify the problems to easier ones without looking like he changed them. He could ace the test, and no one would know how he did it!

He went home that night, and when his dad asked him how the test went, Quincy avoided his eyes and half-heartedly said, "Great!" But he instantly felt a pit in his stomach. He knew what he had done was wrong.

The weekend seemed extra-long to him. He wrestled with what to do. He knew the pit in his stomach wasn't going away for a reason.

Should he tell the truth and apologize? It would be easy to let it go. But he wasn't sure he could live with that awful feeling inside of him that was becoming more uncomfortable with every minute that passed.

On Monday, he told his dad he felt too sick to attend school. His father leaned in and touched his forehead. "Quincy, is there something you want to discuss? You haven't been yourself all weekend."

Quincy's eyes filled with tears. His father sat with him as he cried, and eventually, he opened up to his dad and explained how he had changed all the math problems.

"I see," Dad said. "Well, what can you do to make this right?"

They formulated a plan that involved meeting with Miss Stewart, apologizing, and facing the consequences of his mistake.

Interestingly, even though this was the part he dreaded the most when he thought about telling the truth all weekend, it wasn't as bad as he had imagined, and the pit in his stomach was gone. He actually looked forward to setting things right no matter how hard the consequences were because that seemed better than how he had felt all weekend.

He sat with Miss Stewart and admitted what he had done. They worked together to figure out the next steps.

It seems you can erase your math problems, but you can't erase the feelings that arise from dishonesty unless you do the right thing and mend your mistakes.

DISCUSSION QUESTIONS

- How did Quincy's dad know something was wrong?

- What was surprising to you in the story?

- How do you know Quincy did the right thing in telling his dad?

- What ways could Quincy make things right with Miss Stewart?

- What could have happened if Quincy hadn't told the truth?

SKILL PRACTICE

Let students know that apologies are the foundation of how we restore broken relationships.

Step 1: Direct students to pair up, student 1 chooses a scenario, student 2 chooses a positive response, and student 1 chooses an acceptance.

Step 2: Direct students to pair up, student 1 chooses a scenario, student 2 chooses a negative response, and student 1 chooses an acceptance.

Step 3: Discuss the differences between the two types of responses and how they feel while going through the process. Discuss the best solutions and the reasons why they are the most effective.

Scenarios:

- Your friend chose to go with another friend after school rather than with you as promised.

- A sibling tells something embarrassing about you to their whole class.

- Your caregiver forgot to pack your sports uniform for your game after school, so you can't play.

- Your classmate copied your homework and told the teacher you were the one who cheated.

- Your sibling spilled juice on your brand-new bedspread.

- Your teacher forgot to let you help with the lesson as promised.

- Your caregiver didn't get the school supplies you needed like they said they would do.

- Your sibling forgot to care for her dog, who chewed your favorite hat.

- Your friend got angry with you and said some hurtful things.

Positive Responses:

- I am sorry I....

- It was my fault that _____ happened. I apologize for letting it happen.

- I realize that...

- I realize that _____ was my fault, and I am sorry for making you feel_____.

- I am genuinely sorry that I did this. I want to make things better. How can I do that?

- I am so sorry. Here is my plan on how to make things right...

Negative Responses:

- I am not sorry; I would do it again.

- It was your fault that _____ happened. I don't apologize.

- Whatever!

- You made me feel horrible, and I want you to feel that way too.

- I can tell you aren't sorry.

- I will never forgive you.

Acceptances:

- I accept your apology.

- I'll accept your apology because...

- I felt _____ when that happened. Thank you for apologizing.

- Thank you for apologizing; I still need to think about it. I am feeling....

Non-Acceptances:

- I will NEVER accept your apology.

- You don't deserve forgiveness EVER.

- I want you to suffer.

- You should be ashamed of yourself.

ADDITIONAL ACTIVITIES

- Teach students that we can strengthen our self-awareness skills by sharing things about ourselves. Sharing an "UP" is something you do well and are proud of yourself for, and it makes you happy when you talk about it. Sharing a "HOPE" is something you want to get better at and strengthen and grow capabilities in.

- Let students know that imagining what they could have done differently helps them plan and prepare for future decisions. Have them imagine a situation they wish they could change in time. Have them imagine precisely what they would do differently and then travel to the future, imagining how things are different because they changed the past. Students may want to share or keep their thoughts private.

CLOSING CONSIDERATIONS

Teach students that it is okay to make mistakes and ask for forgiveness, and it is also OK to consider forgiving others when they have done you wrong. It's not easy, but there are many benefits. Forgiving someone has been shown to promote a balanced heart rate and help you breathe better. It has also been shown to help increase mental alertness, lower stress, and release tight muscles.

Ask students to summarize the content of this session's lesson into a single sentence. The student will then consider how they will practice apologizing, repairing their mistakes, and forgiving others when ready throughout this week. In pairs or groups of three, students may share their answers. If time allows, a few students may share with the whole group.

Playing the "Would You Rather?" game is a fun and engaging activity for students to develop their critical thinking skills. Students will reflect on their experience, evaluate their options based on their preferences, and reflect on the opinions of others, providing a different perspective and strengthening their sense of connection to one another.

WOULD YOU RATHER?

Copy and cut out the questions for small groups to discuss, or have each person stand in the center of the room and move towards one side or the other to show their vote for either option as the facilitator reads the questions aloud.

WOULD YOU RATHER RETURN TO A TIME MACHINE SO THAT IT NEVER HAPPENED OR LEARN FROM YOUR MISTAKE?

WOULD YOU RATHER FORGIVE YOURSELF OR FORGIVE OTHERS?

WOULD YOU RATHER FORGIVE SOMEONE YOU FELT DIDN'T DESERVE IT OR WAIT UNTIL THE TIME WAS RIGHT?

WOULD YOU RATHER TALK IT OUT WITH A FRIEND OR PRETEND IT DIDN'T HAPPEN?

WOULD YOU RATHER GIVE SOMEONE A SECOND CHANCE OR WAIT TO SEE IF THEY LEARN THEIR LESSON?

WOULD YOU RATHER DECIDE HOW TO CORRECT THE SITUATION OR ASK AN ADULT FOR HELP?

I can say sorry, acknowledge what happened, and plan a path forward.

EMOTiONS ARE CONTAGiOUS

MIND MAP

On the board, draw a mind map and ask students to consider the meaning of *contagious*.

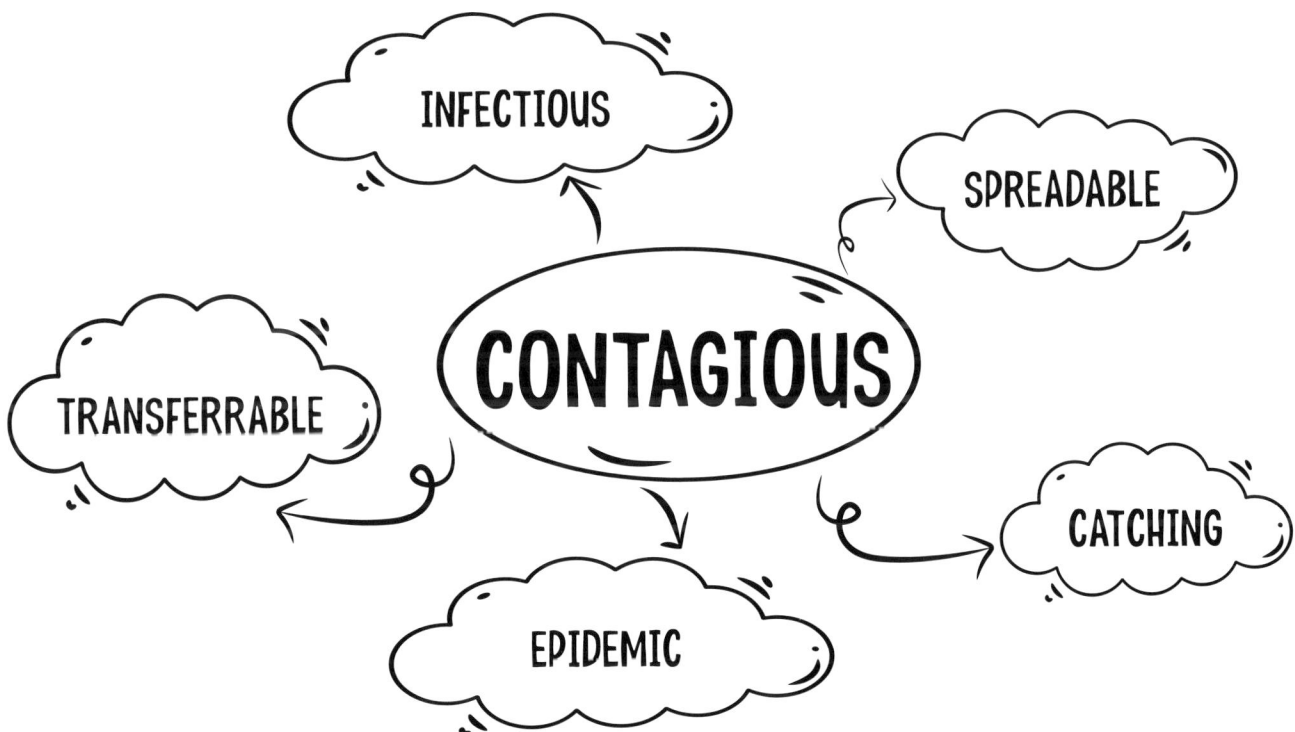

INFECTIOUS

SPREADABLE

TRANSFERRABLE

CONTAGIOUS

CATCHING

EPIDEMIC

ASCA® STANDARDS

- **B-SMS 7.** Effective coping skills
- **B-SS 2.** Positive, respectful, and supportive relationships with students who are similar to and different from them
- **B-SS 4.** Empathy
- **B-SS 9.** Social maturity and behaviors appropriate to the situation and environment

In a small group format, complete a brief check-in with students by asking them to indicate their feelings using the brain stoplight check-in.

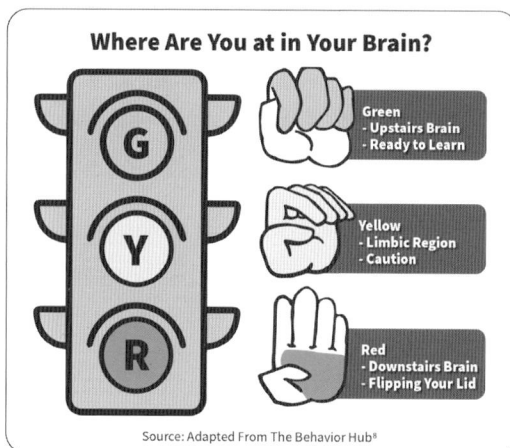

Where Are You at in Your Brain?

Green
- Upstairs Brain
- Ready to Learn

Yellow
- Limbic Region
- Caution

Red
- Downstairs Brain
- Flipping Your Lid

Source: Adapted From The Behavior Hub®

Review the Group Expectations before asking students to share their knowledge of the topic from the previous week. Ask students to share one thing they did differently this past week because of what they learned in last week's lesson. Together, review the Mind Map. Then, read the Lesson Introduction and ask the Circle Time Questions before reading the Story and asking the Discussion Questions. Students can work in pairs to craft their responses or share with the whole group. Complete the Skill Practice, "Would You Rather?" game, and Additional Activities as time allows. Be sure to complete the Closing Considerations with each lesson.

LESSON INTRODUCTION

Have you ever noticed that a smile from someone can brighten up one person's day or even a whole room full of people? Or how hearing someone laugh can bring a smile to your face and put you in a good mood? Emotions are contagious! And just like feelings of Happy and Joy can spread, so can Fear, Sad and Mad.

Pause and consider what emotions you are reflecting to others. Are you spreading those feelings? What emotions are being reflected toward you? Are you catching those feelings?

CIRCLE TIME QUESTIONS

Ask students to reflect and share their answers to the following questions with the group. Larger groups may need to be broken into smaller groups to give students ample time to share their answers and deepen the conversation.

- Have you ever been affected by other people's moods? Explain.

- Do you think you have ever affected other people's moods by how you are feeling? Explain.

- Is it easy to "catch" other people's emotions? Give an example.

Hand out coloring sheets and crayons or markers to younger students while the facilitator reads the story, if desired.

Catching Baseballs and Emotions!

Joey had been best friends with Max since Max's family moved in next door a few years ago. They liked baseball and pizza and had the best time together watching their big brothers play ball.

They both dreamed of making the school baseball team so they could be teammates, and their little brothers could watch them play just like they did with their older siblings.

On the day of tryouts, Max was so nervous that he told Joey he wasn't sure if he could go through with it. Max started shaking and talking fast. Joey's mouth became dry, and he started worrying too as doubt crept in. He noticed that Max's nervousness was starting to rub off on him. He wasn't sure how to help Max and do his best at tryouts until he remembered something he learned from the school counselor, Mr. Painter.

Mr. Painter told Joey that when he gets scared, he imagines the worry as a red balloon and tells the balloon to "float as far away possible." Joey had thought it was kind of silly when Mr. Painter first said it because talking to a balloon seemed a bit ridiculous, but now it was all that came to his mind when he tried to think about how to help, so he decided it wouldn't hurt to give it a shot. Mr. Painter said that to help someone relax and feel calm, you have to be relaxed and steady yourself.

Joey took a deep breath and planted himself firmly on the ground. He told Max all about the balloon, and Max laughed, "Well, only if I can make the balloon blue 'cause I was feeling blue." Joey laughed, too, and they both agreed to send the blue balloon floating away.

Max gave Joey a fist bump and thanked him for shifting his mood. "I guess all I can do is my very best and leave the rest up to the coach." Joey agreed as they walked onto the field together.

DISCUSSION QUESTIONS

- How did Joey avoid catching Max's nervousness?

- Why did Joey take a deep breath before talking to Max?

- How do we know that Max caught Joey's emotions?

- What are the possible emotional outcomes of the tryouts?

- What could have happened if Joey became nervous, too?

SKILL PRACTICE

Using the round-robin method, go around the table and ask students how they would practice each skill, giving every student a chance to answer one question. Skill practiced can be adapted to allow students to respond in pairs or write their answers on scratch paper.

How Would You Practice Spreading Positivity If:

- A classmate walked into the room and complained about the teacher?

- A family member was angry with you for not helping them out?

- A neighbor asked if he could borrow your bike but never returned it?

- Your best friend was upset because of something that happened to them?

- Your teacher gave extra credit to everyone for trying their best except for you?

- Your sibling refused to help you do your chores?

- Your friend invited everyone in the class to their birthday party except for you?

- Your parent bought you new shoes, but you don't like the color or style?

- You overhear kids swearing in the hallways?

- Your least favorite lunch is being served today?

ADDITIONAL ACTIVITIES

- Have students take turns acting out an emotion, while students take turns guessing the emotion.

- Have students come up with new emojis by creatively drawing emotions.

CLOSING CONSIDERATIONS

There will be moments when we make mistakes and others aren't ready to talk it through and forgive us. Don't let that hurt become contagious. Those can be challenging moments to navigate. It's not fun when others are angry or frustrated with us, but we can't control other people's responses, only our own. But we can reflect hope, forgiveness, and positivity that can be contagious.

Ask students to summarize the content of this session's lesson into a single sentence. Students will then consider how they will practice positive emotional contagion throughout this week. In pairs or groups of three, students may share their answers. If time allows, a few students may share with the whole group.

Playing the "Would You Rather?" game is a fun and engaging activity for students to develop their critical thinking skills. Students will reflect on their experience, evaluate their options based on their preferences, and reflect on the opinions of others, providing a different perspective and strengthening their sense of connection to one another.

WOULD YOU RATHER?

Copy and cut out the questions for small groups to discuss, or have each person stand in the center of the room and move towards one side or the other to show their vote for either option as the facilitator reads the questions aloud.

WOULD YOU RATHER MAKE OTHERS SMILE OR NOT SHOW YOUR EMOTIONS?

WOULD YOU RATHER SPREAD HAPPINESS OR MISERY?

WOULD YOU RATHER BE THE RECIPIENT OF POSITIVITY OR A SPREADER?

WOULD YOU RATHER SHARE YOUR FEELINGS ALOUD OR WRITE ABOUT THEM?

WOULD YOU RATHER COMBAT NEGATIVITY THROUGH DISCUSSION OR BY IGNORING IT?

WOULD YOU RATHER BE KNOWN FOR JOINING A GROUP NO MATTER HOW NEGATIVE THEIR WORDS ARE OR TAKING A STAND AGAINST THE NEGATIVITY?

LET WORRIES FLOAT AWAY

Final Group Session

LAST SESSION:
Directions & Overview

The final session is recommended but optional. You may conclude the group during the final lesson topic if time does not permit this final session.

Directions: This final session is more relaxed and carefree, allowing students to spend time with one another and process their feelings about the group's conclusion. Facilitators may provide structured games or allow students unstructured time together.

Post-Group Expectations: Many students will have grown accustomed to meeting with you and will need reassurance about what support will be available after the group's conclusion. Be sure to review the protocol for meeting with you once the group has concluded.

Pre- and Post-Group Survey: Ask students to complete the post-group survey. Review the directions aloud. Discreetly ensure that all questions are answered when the forms are returned.

Certificate of Completion: Present each student with their own Certificate of Completion. You can have as much or as little fanfare around this experience as you would like. Playing a song and asking students to stand and clap for their peers creates lasting memories for the participants.

Group Completion Letter: Give each student their Group Completion Letter to share with their parent or guardian, notifying them that the group has officially ended.

Group Conclusion: Ask each student to share what, if anything, this group has meant to them. Model this activity by sharing your experience as the group's facilitator.

Note to Facilitators: If your district allows it, a group meal is often a fun experience for the students. If you cannot purchase a meal within the district budget, perhaps students could buy their lunches. Be sure to have caregiving permission and be familiar with students' allergies before providing food.

THE RESOURCES IN THIS BOOK ARE AVAILABLE FOR YOU AS A DIGITAL DOWNLOAD!

Please visit **ncyi.org/downloadable-resources**
to access the downloadable resources.

Enter the code below to unlock the resources.:

BIGEMOTIONS563

GRADE LEVEL

The curriculum is ideal for 2nd through 8th grade students.

GROUP TOPICS

My Upstairs and
  Downstairs Brain
Sensing My Senses
Self-Compassion
Safe and Positive
  Relationships
Braving Big Emotions

Stress Busting
Anchors
First Aid for Feelings
Mending Mistakes
Emotions are
  Contagious

10-12 Group Sessions — **30 MIN**

CURRICULUM & MATERIALS

Curriculum:
Use this Managing Big Emotions Workbook to facilitate your groups.

Materials:
Copies of surveys, coloring sheets, and "Would You Rather?" game. Crayons, pencils, and scratch paper.

ASCA® STUDENT BEHAVIOR STANDARDS 19

B-LS 2.
B-LS 3.
B-LS 4.
B-LS 9.
B-SMS 1.
B-SMS 2.
B-SMS 4.
B-SMS 6.
B-SMS 7.
B-SMS 8.
B-SMS 9.
B-SMS 10.
B-SS 1.
B-SS 2.
B-SS 3.
B-SS 4.
B-SS 5.
B-SS 8.
B-SS 9.

NUMBER OF STUDENTS AFFECTED

Small group is ideal for up to six students. Fewer students if goals are related to behavioral issues.

Managing Big Emotionss can be used for classroom lessons.

PERCEPTION DATA

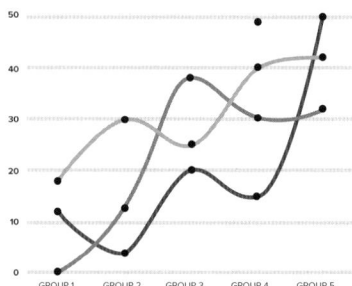

Use Managing Big Emotions survey data to create a visual representation of their progress using their pre- and post-data.

OUTCOME DATA

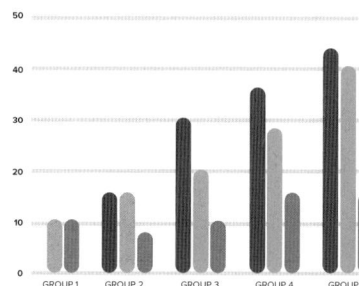

Use achievement, attendance, and behavior data to measure the progress of your students. Compare pre- and post-group impacts.

MANAGING BIG EMOTIONS GROUP PERMISSION FORM

Greetings, Caregivers of: _____,

This form invites your student to attend a Managing Big Emotions Group. Our counseling department offers various services, including class lessons, small groups, and individual sessions with students. There are lots of reasons we invite students to attend groups. We invite students who might need help connecting with their peers, managing conflict or big emotions, improving their grades, or simply because their involvement will allow them to be more successful in their education journey. Your student is not in trouble, and being part of this group is meant to be a positive time for all attendees.

This group will focus on learning about our brains and nervous systems and how we can handle, modulate, and navigate our feelings. We will discuss safe and positive relationships, mending mistakes, how our emotions are contagious, awareness of our senses, and more. Small groups are a fun way for students to learn valuable skills and connect with peers.

We will meet for approximately thirty minutes during the school day _____ times per week. I will work with your child's teacher to select an appropriate time that minimizes interruptions to their learning. When the student has completed all the group sessions, they will receive a Certificate of Completion.

I am excited to work with your child. Please don't hesitate to contact me with any questions or concerns.

Warm Regards,

- -

Please complete and return by: _____

Student's Name: _____

Teacher's Name: _____

☐ YES, I agree to allow my child to attend the Managing Big Emotions Group.

☐ NO, I do NOT agree to allow my child to attend the Managing Big Emotions Group.

_____
Signature of Caregiver

MANAGING BIG EMOTIONS GROUP EXPECTATIONS

CONFIDENTIALITY

In our group, we will keep what we talk about confidential. Confidentiality means keeping what is said in the group private and not discussing it outside of the group. We know that some things are private, and not everyone needs to know about them. However, because we are a group, we can't promise that everyone will keep what you say private, so please be mindful of what you share with the group. If you share that you plan to hurt yourself or someone else or that someone is hurting you, it is my duty to help keep you safe which involves telling someone who needs to know and can keep you and others safe, as well.

SAFETY

We create an environment of physical and emotional safety.
We don't make fun of others and watch out for each other.

ASK FOR HELP WHEN NEEDED

This is a safe place to ask questions and receive help.

LISTEN TO EACH OTHER

Listen from your heart. This is a space to be open, truthful, and respectful. Everyone belongs, and everyone will have a turn. When others are speaking, we can listen with full attention.

HELP OTHERS WHEN WE CAN

It is okay to disagree, but we won't yell or call each other names.
We can support each other in keeping the space safe.

DO OUR BEST

When we fully dive into listening and participating, we will get more out of the group and grow emotionally stronger.

CREATE YOUR OWN

_____

_____

Group Attendance Form

Group:_____ Day/Time:_____

	1	2	3	4	5	6	7	8	9	10	11	12
DATE												
	☐	☐	☐	☐	☐	☐	☐	☐	☐	☐	☐	☐
	☐	☐	☐	☐	☐	☐	☐	☐	☐	☐	☐	☐
	☐	☐	☐	☐	☐	☐	☐	☐	☐	☐	☐	☐
	☐	☐	☐	☐	☐	☐	☐	☐	☐	☐	☐	☐
	☐	☐	☐	☐	☐	☐	☐	☐	☐	☐	☐	☐
	☐	☐	☐	☐	☐	☐	☐	☐	☐	☐	☐	☐
	☐	☐	☐	☐	☐	☐	☐	☐	☐	☐	☐	☐

SESSION 1

SESSION 2

SESSION 3

SESSION 4

SESSION 5

SESSION 6

SESSION 7

SESSION 8

SESSION 9

SESSION 10

SESSION 11

SESSION 12

Group Attendance Form (Example)

Group: 5th Grade Lunch   **Day/Time:** Thursday@12:30

	1	2	3	4	5	6	7	8	9	10	11	12
DATE	3/2	3/9	3/16	3/23								
Jane/Ms. W's Class	X	X	X	X	X	X	X	X	X	X	X	X
George/Mr. Day's Class	X	X		X	X	X	X	X	X	X	X	X
Sami/Ms. Smith's Class	X	X	X	X	X	X	X	X	X	X	X	X
John/Ms. Lee's Class	X		X	X	X	X	X	X	X	X	X	X
Malik/Ms. Lee's Class	X	X	X		X	X		X	X	X	X	X
Prishna/Ms. Smith's Class	X	X	X	X	X	X	X	X	X	X	X	X

SESSION 1	Intro/Surveys/Group Rules and Norms/Discussed expectations/Played game.
SESSION 2	My Upstairs and Downstairs Brain
SESSION 3	Sensing My Senses
SESSION 4	Self-Compassion
SESSION 5	Safe and Positive Relationships
SESSION 6	Braving Big Emotions
SESSION 7	Stress Busting
SESSION 8	Anchors
SESSION 9	First Aid for Feelings
SESSION 10	Mending Mistakes
SESSION 11	Emotions are Contagious
SESSION 12	Check-ins/Post-Group Survey/Process group experience & Certificates awarded.

Pre- and Post-Group Survey

My name is:_____

Date:_____

Managing Big Emotions Survey Pre-/Post-

Circle 👍 if the statement is **true** for you.

Circle 👎 if the statement is **NOT true** for you.

There are no right or wrong answers!

I can usually figure out why I am feeling big emotions.	👍	👎
I can usually tell when I need to be alone and allow myself to calm down.	👍	👎
I can usually figure out if a person is a safe and positive influence.	👍	👎
I can usually figure out what helps lessen my stress.	👍	👎
I can usually figure out what or who helps me handle my feelings.	👍	👎
I can usually figure out how to return to a relaxed state after feeling overwhelmed.	👍	👎
I can usually figure out what my nervous system and senses are trying to tell me.	👍	👎
I can usually show myself compassion when I am overwhelmed by saying "no" to others who are wanting my help.	👍	👎
I usually know what works for me when I need a break or something else to feel better.	👍	👎
I usually know how to handle it when I make a mistake.	👍	👎
I can usually recognize when someone's emotions are rubbing off on me.	👍	👎

Anything else you would like to share about the group? Write it below.

_____

_____

Post-Group Survey Results

Managing Big Emotions Group Data

GROUP GOAL:

STUDENT STATEMENTS:

GPA Results

Increase the total GPA following group intervention for group participation by ____%

____%

Attendance Results

Decrease the number of absences by ____% following group intervention for group participants

____%

Discipline Results

Decrease the number of conduct referrals by ____% following group intervention

____%

STUDENTS ATTENDED

NUMBER OF SESSIONS

OVERALL IMPROVEMENT

(See Formula Lower Right)

☐ Pre-Group % True   ◼ Post-Group % True

0

I can usually figure out why I am feeling big emotions.

I can usually tell when I need to be alone and allow myself to calm down.

I can usually figure out if a person is a safe and positive influence.

I can usually figure out what helps lessen my stress.

I can usually figure out what or who helps me handle my feelings.

I can usually figure out how to return to a relaxed state after feeling overwhelmed.

I can usually figure out what my nervous system and senses are trying to tell me.

I can usually show myself compassion when I am overwhelmed by saying "no" to others who are wanting my help.

I usually know what works for me when I need a break or something else to feel better.

I usually know how to handle it when I make a mistake.

I can usually recognize when someone's emotions are rubbing off on me.

OVERALL IMPROVEMENT FORMULA

$$\left(\frac{\text{Post-Group Total} - \text{Pre-Group Total}}{\text{Pre-Group Total}} \right) \times 100$$

Managing Big Emotions Group Data

GROUP GOAL:

Reduce the number of discipline referrals by 10% for a group of six students who had more than three discipline referrals last year.

STUDENT STATEMENTS:

"I really like coming to group."

"I learned how to talk about my big feelings."

"I am not the only person who feels this way sometimes."

"I think I can be a better friend now."

"I can dig deeper to find out what's under my anger."

GPA Results

Increase the total GPA following group intervention for group participation by __5__%

5 %

Attendance Results

Decrease the number of absences by __53__% following group intervention for group participants

53 %

Discipline Results

Decrease the number of conduct referrals by __42__% following group intervention

42 %

STUDENTS ATTENDED

6

NUMBER OF SESSIONS

12

OVERALL IMPROVEMENT

63.15%

(See Formula Lower Right)

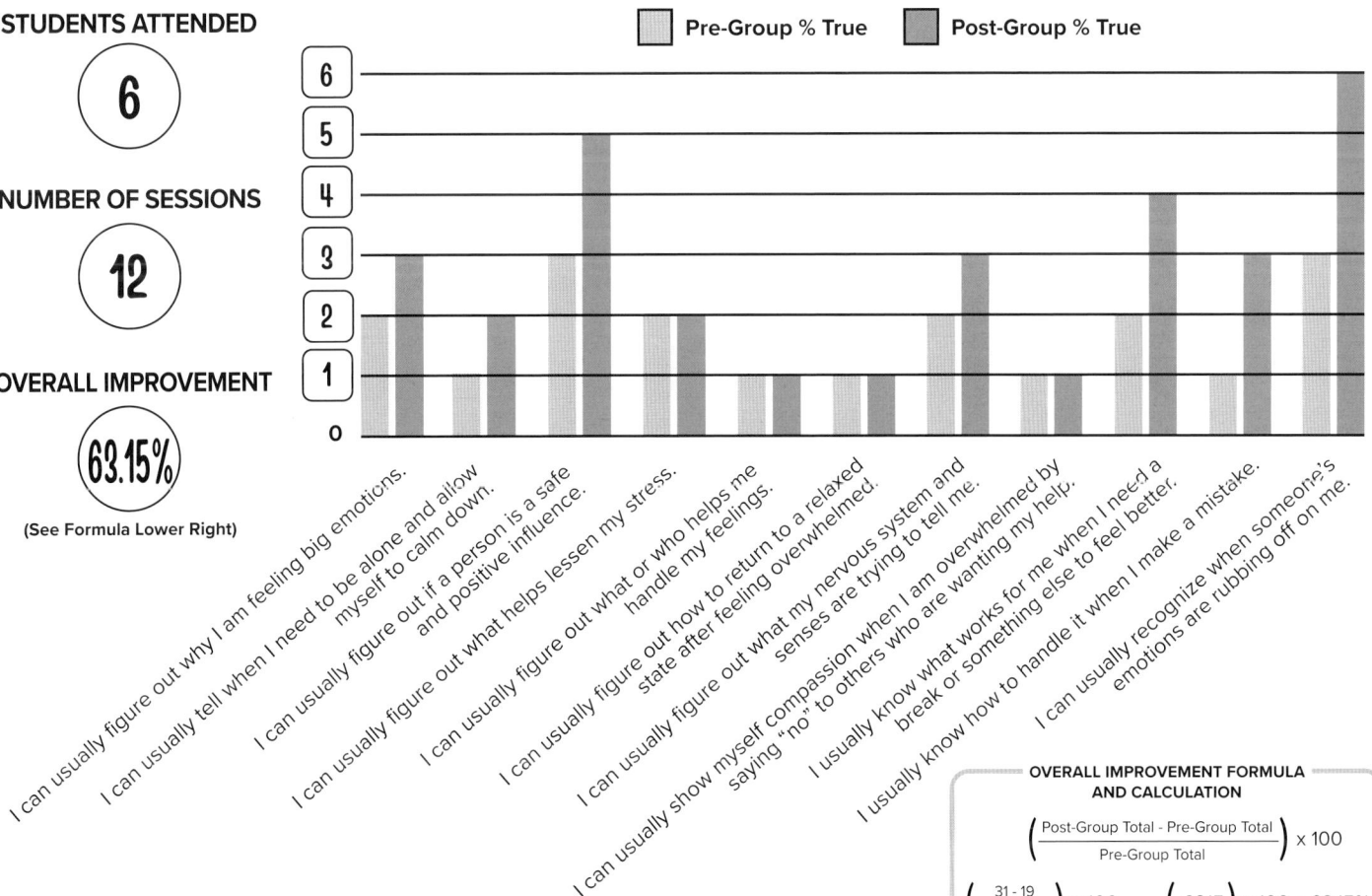

Pre-Group % True   **Post-Group % True**

Bar chart (0–6) comparing Pre-Group % True and Post-Group % True for statements:
- I can usually figure out why I am feeling big emotions.
- I can usually tell when I need to be alone and allow myself to calm down.
- I can usually figure out if a person is a safe and positive influence.
- I can usually figure out what helps lessen my stress.
- I can usually figure out what or who helps me handle my feelings.
- I can usually figure out how to return to a relaxed state after feeling overwhelmed.
- I can usually figure out what my nervous system and senses are trying to tell me.
- I can usually show myself compassion when I am overwhelmed by saying "no" to others who are wanting my help.
- I usually know what works for me when I need a break or something else to feel better.
- I usually know how to handle it when I make a mistake.
- I can usually recognize when someone's emotions are rubbing off on me.

OVERALL IMPROVEMENT FORMULA AND CALCULATION

$$\left(\frac{\text{Post-Group Total} - \text{Pre-Group Total}}{\text{Pre-Group Total}} \right) \times 100$$

$$\left(\frac{31 - 19}{19} \right) \times 100 \qquad \left(.6315 \right) \times 100 = 63.15\%$$

30-MINUTE GROUPS

CERTIFICATE OF COMPLETION

This Certificate is Presented to:

_____

For Participating in the **Managing Big Emotions Group!**

Facilitator: _____

WAY TO GO!

MANAGING BIG EMOTIONS GROUP COMPLETION LETTER

Date:_____

Hello!

Today was the final session in our Managing Big Emotions Group, and we wanted to let you know that your student has been presented with a Certificate of Completion.

Over the past ten sessions, we have reviewed the following topics:

- My Upstairs and Downstairs Brain

- Sensing My Senses

- Self-Compassion

- Safe and Positive Relationships

- Braving Big Emotions

- Stress Busting

- Anchors

- First Aid for Feelings

- Mending Mistakes

- Emotions are Contagious

I am still their counselor and will still be available to them as needed. However, we will no longer be meeting every week. Please don't hesitate to contact me with any questions or concerns.

I am so proud of them and excited they were able to attend. Thank you so much for allowing them to participate in our Managing Big Emotions Group!

Warm regards,

_____

School Counselor

ENDNOTES

1   Jessica Sinarski and Macky Pamintuan, *Hello Anger: A Picture Book About Figuring Out What's Underneath Your Angry Feelings* (Chattanooga, TN: National Center for Youth Issues, 2022).

2   Daniel J. Siegel and Tina Payne Bryson, *The Whole-Brain Child: 12 Revolutionary Strategies to Nurture Your Child's Developing Mind* (New York: Bantam, 2012).

ABOUT THE AUTHOR

Ginger Healy MSW, LCSW is a clinical social worker with almost 30 years of experience in the field of social work. Ginger has worked as a child abuse investigator, hospital social worker, and school therapist. She spent 15 years as the social service supervisor at an international adoption agency and was able to travel to provide support for orphanages all over the world. This job taught her so much about attachment and trauma needs in children. She currently works as the program director for the Attachment and Trauma Network where she co-anchors the podcast "Regulated & Relational" and speaks across the nation on trauma-informed schools, therapeutic parenting, and community engagement. She is also the author of *15-Minute Focus: Regulation and Co-Regulation* and an accompanying workbook, along with *30-Minute Groups: Managing Big Emotions*. She is married with four children who have been her greatest teachers about developmental trauma and special needs. Ginger loves to travel and is an avid reader.

Connect with Ginger at
attachmenttraumanetwork.org

A Brief Look at Ginger's Workshop Sessions

Emotional Regulation and Co-Regulation for the Classroom

Ginger brings hope into classrooms by teaching the importance of educator regulation and co-regulation strategies. Ginger makes neuroscience accessible and shares the three steps of the regulation cycle that can bring calm and healing into the classroom. She demonstrates how regulation of the educator's nervous system is crucial in managing the behaviors and big feelings in the classroom while sharing easy-to-implement strategies that can work for any child. This session will empower educators to lower the stress levels of both students and themselves.

Trauma-Informed Education

Ginger discusses and explains trauma-sensitive schools – what they are and what the paradigm shift surrounding them looks like. She helps attendees understand the pervasiveness of trauma and its impact on student learning and teaches how to recognize the signs and respond with a trauma-sensitive approach to avoid re-traumatization. This session will provide participants with strategies to implement in the classroom that support students through safety, regulation, and connection.

Neuroplasticity: We Can Change Brains!

Ginger makes neuroscience fascinating and fun as she explores strategies that re-wire a child's brain from chaos to calm. Ginger gives an experiential lesson on the hand- brain model that empowers children to manage their feelings and behaviors, moving them out of shame and into post-traumatic growth. This session will introduce participants to brain basics that are essential to understanding in order to shape educator response to behaviors.

ncyionline.org/speakers

For the Givers: Preventing Burnout for Educators

What exactly is burnout? How do you know when you are approaching it, and can it be avoided? Ginger explores self-care and community care strategies while teaching how to complete the stress cycle. Ginger will teach research-based implementations that can be put into place immediately and will help educators start on the road to healing. This session is dedicated to "all the givers" who will walk away inspired and energized with a concrete plan to move forward.

Creating Calm Kits and Regulation Rooms

Ginger discusses the importance of "felt-safety" and creating safe spaces in the classroom and throughout the entire school building. Ginger will break down how to create a calm kit and regulation room and will also share dos and don'ts for each. Participants will walk away with a How-To formula, including a list of rules, a list of supplies, and a new lens of thinking when it comes to behavior management.

The Importance of Relationships: Connecting with Hard-to-Reach Students

Ginger discusses attachment- what it is, how it's developed, and why it's important for academic success. She explores buffer relationships and attunement to student needs. She digs into teacher triggers and how to look at behaviors that get under our skin. Ginger will offer strategies for removing barriers that block academic success and emotional healing. Participants will make a paradigm shift in understanding behaviors and be able to implement strategies to help children reach academic success and get on the path to healing adversities.

ncyionline.org/speakers

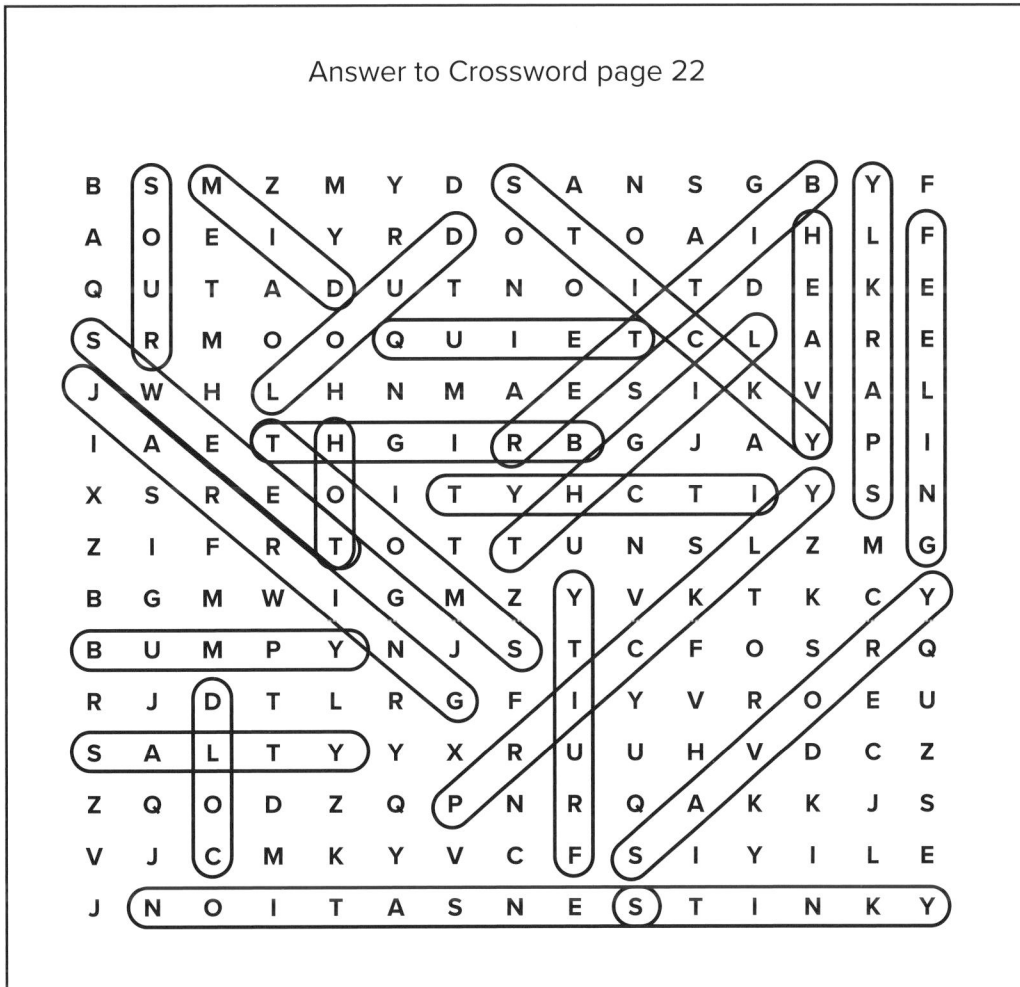

Answer to Crossword page 22

NATIONAL CENTER for YOUTH ISSUES

About NCYI

National Center for Youth Issues provides educational resources, training, and support programs to foster the healthy social, emotional, and physical development of children and youth. Since our founding in 1981, NCYI has established a reputation as one of the country's leading providers of teaching materials and training for counseling and student-support professionals. NCYI helps meet the immediate needs of students throughout the nation by ensuring those who mentor them are well prepared to respond across the developmental spectrum.

Connect With Us Online!

@nationalcenterforyouthissues

@ncyi

@nationalcenterforyouthissues